Apocalypse 2012: God's Judgments

Apocalypse 2012: God's Judgments

Ernest Johnson

To order additional copies of this book, contact:
Xlibris Corporation
1-888-795-4274
www.Xlibris.com
Orders@Xlibris.com
117589

CONTENTS

APOCALYPSE
SEVEN SEAL JUDGMENTS

Time frame: The first seal portrays the Second Coming of Christ in the air. This is referring to the rapture of the church. If this is true, then these seal judgments will begin at the very beginning of the tribulation period. The fifth seal, however pictures the martyrdom and the prosecution of the believers during this tribulation period. When does this occur?

At the point of the tribulation period when Jesus says to the Jews to flee to the mountains, this is the time when the fifth seal would occur. They are told to flee at midpoint of the tribulation. This is after the beast kills the two super prophets of God and after the antichrist enters the temple. He will announce that God is dead or there is no God. This shows us that the fifth and the sixth seal judgments provide an overview of the entire seven-year period of the tribulation period on the earth.

First I want to state right up front that there is not any one interpretation of these events. All end time writers look through the lens of Prophecy to see the world. I will at times attempt to do the exact opposite. Look at prophecy through the eyes of the world. They are all skeptical in there view points. Nothing is written in stone. Nothing is for sure. The events that unfold in this heavenly scene is just that, it is the view in heaven and the way they see things are not clear at all to man. Revelation reveals an angelic war and their judgments. Man kind has a thick veil over his eyes of deception and this prevents him of seeing things that are outlined in the book of Revelation. So no matter what the best of scholars say it is only one interpretation. So Do I have the right answer? Why yes I do. I have all of the lousy view points at my finger tips right here at my disposal. I have viewed them all. I have to say that I am severely disappointed in my review material. "The history of the world is God's judgment of the world". Don't ask me where I found this phrase because like all the things I say I can't remember where I got them. I have in my head all kinds of things I have collected over time. Perhaps Those other writers and along with the educated elite will think me loony. Well my response is this. Well yes, I do watch my share of loony tunes.

Again I will state if not for the first time in my other material that man kind doesn't really know shit about anything, not really. The scriptures say that man thinks in part and knows in part. We have to rely on each other in this universe to get the larger picture of any one subject. After all, this is not only the same message of Christ at the parable of the two sinners praying. It is also the parable of the secret societies that say you don't know that you don't know. This is the exact same view of the god's 'man doesn't know god damn shit". Not individually any way. But collectively we can get the greater picture of all things. The will of the god's is the one that actually counts. We humans play out their desire to the world's end unknowingly. Humans are just pawns in the board game.

Mainly there are four ways to view things. The first being the Historicist. The second is the Preterist view of things. The third is the Futurist view of things. The fourth is the Spiritual view of things. These views I will bounce in and out of as I see fit that will help us determine things in there proper perspective according to my taste. So in the end I will give just as a distorted view as all the rest. Are you confused? You should be. One thing that I need you to understand about me, as I reviewed my material before hand I first eat it then I digest it as best I can and then I puke it back up. So as I write I am puking at the same time. Sick, isn't it? Let's begin.

Historicist Approach This is the historic Protestant interpretation of the book and sees the Book of Revelation as a prewritten record of the course of history from the time of the apostle to the end of the world. Therefore the fulfillment is considered to be in progress at present and has been unfolding for nearly two thousand years.

Preterist Approach The preterist approach sees the fulfillment of Revelation's prophecies as already having occurred in what is now the ancient past, not long after the author's own time. Therefore, the fulfillment was in the future from the point of view of the inspired author, but it is in the past from our vantage point in history. Some preterist believe that the final chapters of Revelation look forward to the second coming of Christ. Others think that everything in the book has reached its culmination in the past.

The Futurist The futurist approach postulates that the majority of the prophecies of the book of Revelation has never yet been fulfilled and await future fulfillment. Futurist interpreters usually apply everything after chapter four to a relatively brief period before the return of Christ.

Spiritual Approach What is called the spiritual approach is often called the idealist or symbolic approach. Revelation does not attempt to find individual fulfillments of the visions but takes Revelation to be a great drama depicting transcendent spiritual realities, such as the spiritual conflict between Christ and Satan, between the saints and the Antichristian world powers, and depicting the heavenly vindication and final Victory of Christ and his saints. Fulfillment is seen either as entirely spiritual or as recurrent, finding representative expression in historical events throughout the age, rather than in one time, specific fulfillments. The prophecy is then rendered applicable to Christians in any age. Let me say right now that the One who is opening these seals is the only one qualified to do so, the Christ Himself.

> **Rev. 5:1-5 Says:** {And I saw in the right hand of Him who sat upon the throne a book written inside and on the back, sealed up with seven seals. * And I saw a strong angel proclaiming with a loud voice, "Who is worthy to open the book, (scroll) and to break its seals?" * And no one in heaven, or on the earth or under the earth, was able to open the book (scroll) or to look into it. * And I began to weep greatly, because no one was found worthy to open the book (scroll} or look into it. * and one of the elders said to me, "Stop weeping: behold, the Lion that is from the tribe of Judah, the Root of David, has overcome so as to open the book (scroll) and its seven seals."}

What this is saying is that Jesus Christ is the One who is doing these judgments. No one else is worthy of this job. We have the King Himself bringing the hammer down by unleashing the great sword on all humanity and unleashing all hell on this earth. This is His time to do so. This is His right alone because He has the title deed to this earth and its time to claim title. He is about to clear the house and the land for his occupation. Who are we to argue? He said during his time on earth that he did not come to bring peace He came to bring a sword. Perhaps this is His way of saying the one who lives by the sword and the one who God hears are the same. It is they who He had in mind. This theory is ludicrous at least, but in light of today's world is makes total sense. This is how I have come to think. I am out there. Also remember that the apostle Paul and the apostle John of Revelation was said to be mentally disordered. They both were mentally unstable to say the least. There is nothing wrong with that. Their penal gland was over active. They were in tune to the eternal vibrations. They were mentally superior. They also were legitimate apostles.

> **Rev. 6:1, 2 Says: {And I saw when the Lamb broke one of the seven seals, and I heard one of the four living creatures saying as with a loud voice of thunder, "Come." * And I looked, and Behold, a white horse, and he who sat on it had a bow; and a crown was given to him; and he went out conquering, and to conquer.}**

Now as an American I can say Hey! This is the United States. Don't think so? Then what is the United States doing right now and has done in the last one hundred years. We have been conquering nations. Maybe God has given the United States a crown. We have definitely marched into the world as peace loving people. We are like a lamb but do speak like a dragon. After all we are a Christian nation from an historical perspective. What does the future look like? Well from my stand point I see the United States on the world march as a future conqueror. Do you see this too? In the future the United States will stand up again and claim its place in world dominance. Perhaps this is not written in prophecy because only that which is pertaining to the Middle East and Israel only matters. There are at least one hundred seventy five nations that are not listed in prophecy. Not surprised that we are not either.

Let me say this. There are the prophecies then there is the reality. The idea is to connect the two with solid reasoning, right? If the gloves fit then you must acquit, savvy? But sadly to say this is not the perspective of the smart professionals. They are schooled in the fine art of interpretation. Let's view their thinking.

One very prominent writer indicates that this rider and his white horse is the Anti-Christ of Rome. The white indicates purity. The crown indicates kingly. The bow indicates intelligent supremacy in war. The United States fits all the above. The United States has become the supreme dictator over more people than any leading nation in the history next to the Roman Empire, which by the way is also the United States.

We have mesmerized people all over the world to worship us. The world has happily bestowed upon us absolute authority over everything. This conqueror carries with him a warriors bow. The arrows of this bow are on the Presidential Seal of the United States. The bow is considered a long range weapon and is symbolic of other long range weapons. America has seduced all the peoples of the earth up to this point. The whole world has claimed America as their savior and benevolent dictator. Tell me this is not so. You know it is. But this is not the view of those in this world. They are still distant on the subject. I will not claim absolute on this view. After all it is only one view. Let me put other's view as more important than mine.

More than one writer has written that this rider is the antichrist. If this is the case then it puts the United States as the earthly for runner of this antichrist if not the antichrist itself. We are living in the land of the antichrist. Then it just to stands to reason we are also living in the land of the kingdom of darkness psychologically. Is this not the case? Most people will answer hell no. But think about this for a moment. Where is this country going right now? It is going to the political dogs. They have the run of things and they are totally screwing things up. Their rules and regulations are putting a tight death grip on everything and every one of us. We are all dying of stagnation here. When the god of this world takes over he is not going to announce that he is the god of this world. He will slip in unannounced and mask him self as a man with good intentions, right? Same thing holds true here. The antichrist is already active through our system of things. Can you feel it?

The same holds true with the return of Christ. It too is an on going event not just a one time event. The heavens are active as we speak. The culmination will unfold but it is all a process. The antichrist is also the same. This is why the world is unfolding as it is. We are not looking at it this way though. We are expecting things to unfold in another manner. This is the earthly deception and the lie. It is unfolding right before our eyes. We just can't see it. We have not made the connection because we are living the lie instead. This is another way of saying we are on the wrong frequency thanks to the world's religions and their heresies. To see it this way you have to train your thinking differently and tap into the reality that is presently there. Get your mind out of the mystical mind set that religion gives. In other words we are lost. Get it! Wake up world. Religion is just another way of being lost.

One writer says that the antichrist will lead the most powerful military alliance in history. Well, again the United States will be at the head of this alliance if not already. Maybe there will be a greater one than one exists now. I think this is the higher view. This is saying we haven't seen anything yet. What do you think it would be like if Western civilization had an alliance with the Middle East Arabs? Is this not America's aim? Thought provoking isn't it?

Let me add this in for good measure. Where was the United States in the world wars? At the top of the food chain that's where. We are a nation that is of peace and we wear a crown and we do speak we speak as a dragon. We are the envy of the world and the whole world has worshiped us. We do have the most powerful military in the history of the planet. We have gone forth and have conquered many nations and this is the business of the United States today. This trend will continue into the future. Those in the world have said "who is like this beast". "Who can make war with him"? Nobody can that's who. But this will change.

> **Rev.6:3, 4 Says: {And when He broke the second seal, I heard the second living creature saying, "Come." * And another, a red horse, went out; and to him who sat on it, it was granted to take peace from the earth, and that men should slay one another; and a great sword was given to him.}**

The second seal is related to war. One writer believes that this time period is during the tribulation. The facts on the earth says that we have been a world at war for the last one hundred years. These are two opposing view points. But if our present age is the tribulation then this would link us together as both being right. Remember there is no one right answer here. I am just putting my two cents in and they are just that, two cents.

Events could mean only that which pertains to the Middle East, unless the Scriptures indicate different. So this Scripture could only refer to what is happening in the current wars there. Men are slaying one another. There has been a low level civil war going on in Iraq for sometime now.

The great sword is interesting. The Arabs are sworn to live and die by the sword. Maybe this is in reference to them. "By your sword you shall live" is the phrase. This is indicative of the Arabs warring nature. There is also a heavy vibration of war going on in Iran at this time. Libya has just fallen to NATO and the rebels working together.

The color of the horse which is red is indicative of bloodshed and speaks of the time when blood shed comes upon the earth. There will be constant tension among nations and the ambitions of men have their climax before the return of Christ. Is this not what is happening in the world today? This has been the case all of my born days. Wars and Rumors of wars have been characteristic of this age. It is evident that warfare plays a large part in the end of the ages with a loss of billions of lives. There is a series of wars on a continuous bases and this trend will continue till the end of time.

Wars are God's judgment for man's sinful nature. Empires established by conquest often dissolve as the result of the lack of unity within. The red horse is indicative of the war within which is civil war. Civil war leads to revolution and revolt. The horrors and carnage of war are God's way of judging sinful societies.

The second horse does also mean a loss of peace. To take peace from the earth can be translated as to deprive all tranquility. This is the spirit of this current world thanks to terrorism. Terrorism is started by Arabs who are carrying this great sword by the way.

I heard it said once that the history of the world is the judgment of the world. Perhaps this is meaning that God is using the Arab's anger to spring on the judgment of God. This would make their statement prophetic and their Jihad against the West unavoidable. After all isn't this their view? The great sword given to this rider is the Machaira, the same word used in Christ's statement cited. It was a short sword or knife suited for the killing of a sacrificial animal, such as that used by Abraham when he intended to slay Isaac. Also the word kill is Sphatto, a word used else where of killing of Christ the Lamb and of whose souls were seen "under the alter." It properly means "slaughter" and thus could point to the sacrificial character of the faithful martyr's deaths.

> **Rev. 6:5, 6 Says: {And when he broke the third seal, I heard the third living creature saying, "Come." And I looked, and behold, a black horse; and he who sat on it had a pair of scales in his hand. * And I heard as it were a voice in the center of the four living creatures saying, "A quart of wheat for a denarius, and three quarts of barley for a denarius; and do not harm the oil and the wine."}**

This black horse is indicating famine. Where there is war there is famine following, while famine means the extreme scarcity of food. This seal is also associated with plagues and diseases.

Many also see this is started by the fiscal oppression imposed by the governments of the times. Taxes are heavy and people are paying through the nose in taxes. In the third century people could pay their taxes in oil, wine or grains. This greatly suggests that this seal is representing general economic deprivation caused by heavy taxation along with oppressive laws. This leads people to deliberately reduce production to avoid large taxation. In ancient times dictators raised real estate taxes to unprecedented levels. Oppressive laws demanded that land be heavily taxed based on its productivity. This led landowners to deliberately reduce grain production to avoid high taxation. This practice of destroying crops to avoid high taxes became so widespread that the government issued an edict forbidding the destruction of olive trees and grapevines, thus coming up with the phrase 'do not harm the oil and the wine".

Once global war breaks out a war with the use of advanced weapons of massive destruction like smart bombs, there are going to be disruptions in the food distribution along with the dislocations in the world economic system. The way the food, electricity medicine and cooking fuel are distributed will be turned into chaos for certain.

Global weather patterns have changed dramatically throughout the last century. Food production is at an all time low. By the year 2025 China will have to have all of the world's grain consumption alone. Imagine what if long periods of a world wide drought would look like? Not only that, but today's seed production have been tampered with. Today's seeds are maybe two of three generation productive. Then they go bad. They have been genetically altered by Monsanto corp.

Diseases have been put under control. But they will be coming back soon. We already have diseases that laugh at antibiotics because of the overuse of antibiotics. In Matt. 24:4-8 Jesus makes reference to famines, plagues and earthquakes in various places. This is saying no telling where they will occur. Plagues are bacterial infections, disastrously evil plagues. They will smother the earth and be spread by planes and the wind. Once the world is consumed by war there will be diseases, plagues, wracked by hunger coupled with economic calamity. The scope of the pandemic is beyond the pandemics already gripping the world is beyond the ability of most of us to understand.

By the year 2000 there have been one hundred million aids cases reported world wide. This is triple what the WTO had predicted. In Asia and Africa combined there is more than 15 million infected. It is also the leading cause of death in Americans between the ages 25 to 45.

Current statistics are as follows: As it is presently two million babies die every year by malnutrition. At least fifty people will have died by the time you have finished reading this chapter. Two hundred twenty five million children worldwide have physical and mental problems due to malnutrition. Not to mention toxic waste in the systems. More than eighty hundred million in this world will go hungry tonight and every night on planet earth. In America the land of the antichrist the richest nation of the earth thirty three million people go to bed hungry; this is one in every six people in this nation.

The country close to us which is Mexico have many more people who are pathetic hungry people eating and sleeping on dirt in a desperate attempt to survive. I have seen this myself in Nogales. More than one billion people on this planet earn less than one dollar per day. These statistics are beyond belief.

When the antichrist comes forth things will get worse in the name of getting better. He will come with the promise to make things better. This is why he will be very popular. We know we are in the tribulation when business and commerce and trading will be totally controlled. In the antichrist's kingdom together with other cooperative nations under his diabolical control, no one will be able to buy or sell unless they have the mark of the beast or 666, which is the number of his name.

> **Rev.6:7, 8 Says: {And when He broke the fourth seal, I heard the voice of the fourth living creature saying, "Come." * And I looked, and behold, an ashen (sickly pale) horse; and he who sat on it had the name death; and Hades was following with him. And authority was given to them over a fourth of the earth, to kill with sword and famine and with pestilence (death) and by the wild beasts of the earth.}**

Let me go over board here and make an out of this world interpretation here. We know that this pale horse is associated with death. Death by war is going on already. But now we will add pestilence with this. Pestilence is defined as plagues. Plagues are defined as destructive contagious bacterial disease. Disastrous evil will befall this world. But what if my claim about the Arabs and the sword are true? What if this is referring to the Muslims? Muslims are strongly associated with the sword. They are about one fourth of the world's population. Maybe this is not true. Maybe one fourth of the world is meaning that this Muslim religion spans one fourth of the world. They also have a religion that is spreading faster than Christianity and are the second largest religion next to Christianity. This trend will definitely continue. They have a hateful grudge and they are on the rise with new technology and we know that that they want to all die. We also know they have been getting baptized in war by warring with each other and now they are uniting against the West. The West knows this and is taking counter measures to bring balance by aligning our selves with the Muslims only to lead them to Armageddon which passes through Jerusalem. Makes sense doesn't it? They are just now coming alive. "Their hand is against everyone and everyone's hand is against them".

Terror is the act of calling up hell. They are calling forth all hell. Now hell will respond in due time. Allah has put it in their hearts to fulfill his purpose. God and Allah are the one and the same here, or it appears so. Remember it is the gods who are controlling things here. God and Satan are the gods. All the gods have one thing they agree on and that is to do what has been decreed from the beginning and that is to bring this age to an end with violence. This is Jehovah's will. All Godly angels and all fallen angels are all working to this very end. This is called cooperative opposition. Hades means hell. The Muslim Jihad is calling forth all hell and that means all that pertains in it. All of the demons as well.

Now in chapter 9 of Revelation we jump ahead and we see during the fifth trumpet the abyss is opened up right away. So we see that Scripture backs up my theory here that hell is on its way.

Hades is the abode of the dead. Perhaps this is the right answer. All hell is not yet unleashed but the abode of the dead are let go. What this is saying to me at the time or this writing the abode of the dead is releasing their captives. The prison walls are coming down. This prison gates are being unlocked. There are human souls there as well as fallen angels there as well. I am sure they have different locations for them all. But maybe the human souls are released at this time. The ones that are supposed to be released any way. Perhaps this is the dead rising to be with the Lord. "The dead in Christ will rise first". Is this theory really out there? I think it is. But it is biblical. Nothing else makes more sense. This is a more realistic stand than all the others that I have read. Now also take note that the theorist know that these events are not in sequential order. So it can very well happen this way. But let's not dismiss all other writers. They are all right in their own way. We are all trying to figure this paradox out.

The word Ishmael means God hears. This could very well mean that God hears the Muslims. So they are absolutely right in their claims that Allah is with them. God uses our tormentors to straighten us out. The word Jacob means one who cheats. We know the Muslims goal is to destroy the one who cheats, Israel.

> **Rev. 6; 9-11 Says: {And when he broke the fifth seal, I saw underneath the alter the souls of those who had been slain because of the word of God, and because of the testimony they had maintained; * and they cried out with a loud voice, saying, "How long, O Lord, holy and true, wilt Thou refrain from judging and avenging our blood on those who dwell on the earth?" *And there was given to each of them a white robe; and they were told that they would rest for a little while longer, until the number of their fellow brethren who were to be killed even as they had been, should be completed also.}**

This seal is associated with the martyrs, those who have already died and those who will die. Those who have died are present are begging God to avenge their blood. But God says in return that they need to rest a little longer and then gave them white robes to wear

So we have those who have died previously which means past tense. Maybe these are the souls that were let go in the fourth seal when hell let go of its captives. If so then these were the people of past history who are waiting in paradise which is the place of separation of those who belong to God and those who do not. We can learn about it in Matthew in the parable of Lazarus. Jesus talks about this place. There is a great gulf between them there. As these souls ascend to heaven they are gathered here underneath the Alter and have not received their orders as of yet. They apparently are newbie's. They are new arrivals. God responds to them by saying "to rest awhile longer". They are to rest until the rest of the brethren have been murdered. So we have a time span here. So God is waiting for all the murdered souls to have come to completion. This is the soul harvest that is taking place. This is an event in time. This is a sequence waiting to be completed. So God does what now? He gives them a white robe. Let's go left with this statement here. Let's try to change the prospective rules. We would normally look at this in the literal sense. They will wear a white garment. I don't think so. I think this white garment is not a piece of clothing. God does not bother with such trivial statements as clothes. What he is referring to here is much different. We cloth ourselves with the words we speak. The garment we wear in our inner lives is the garment of vibration. Our vibrations are a result of our words. Our words are a result of our thinking. Our garment of life is the one we put on every time we speak blessings and curses. Ever hear of the term "Put on the garment of praise?" So we always clothe ourselves in our own words. This is clothing our soul. God does not care about our clothes per say. He sees our soul. The angelic host and the demons know this as well. We humans are ignorant of this perspective. This in turn determines our vibrational energy. All things are energy in heaven and on earth. So it just to stands to reason that this white robe is a new vibration. It is a new tone. We are instruments. We are tones. We are vibrations all singing at different frequencies. Makes sense, does to me. The song of the universe is eternal love. What God is giving them is the White Robe of Love. The heavenly vibrations of love. To bathe in the p-rays. God has swept all bad vibrations from them by forgiving their sins therefore making them white. Does this sound funny? Well, it should. It's not what they teach you in Sunday school.

> **Rev. 7:13, 14 Says: {And one of the elders answered, saying to me, "These who are clothed in the white robes, who are they, and from where have they come?" * And I said to them, "My Lord, you know." And he said to me, "These are the ones who come out of the tribulation, and they have washed their robes and made them white in the blood of the lamb.}**

So what this is saying these tribulation saints has washed their own robes (soul) and made them white. In other words they already had these robes before entering heaven. Again these robes are their souls that have been washed in the blood of the Lamb. The essence of this statement is their vibrational energy has been made pure. There I have made my case. What this means is their belief system is Christ oriented. This is why they are there with Christ. Makes perfect sense to me, go wash your robe.

> **Rev.6:12-17 Says: {And I looked when He broke the sixth seal, and there was a great earthquake; and the sun became as sackcloth made of hair, and the whole moon became like blood; * and the stars of the sky fell to the earth, as a fig tree casts its un ripe figs when shaken by a great wind. *And the sky was split apart like a scroll when it is rolled up; and every mountain and island were moved out of their places. * And the kings of the earth and the great men and the commanders and the rich and the strong and every slave and free man, hid**

**themselves in the caves and among the rocks of the mountain;
* and they said to the mountains and to the rocks, "Fall on us
and hide us from the presence (face) of Him who sits on the
throne, and from the wrath of the Lamb; * for the great day
of their wrath has come; and who is able to stand?"}**

This opening of the sixth seal brings cosmic disturbances. This seal is strongly associated with terror. Shall we say that this scripture is associated with terrorism? Believe me there is something going on here that is greater than terrorism. Acts 10:11, 12 introduces a UFO Vessel. The sky is scrolled back (opened up).

If this is to be taken literally then something has got to happen that will cause this event. Maybe cosmic disturbances will occur in the sixth seal judgment. The first of four earthquakes will occur during the sixth seal in the seven year tribulation. A nuclear exchange is likely as well. Also the arrivals of UFO'S are not out of the question.

But some believe other things and that is not to be taken literally. These are symbolic signs only. They still have representation. Like maybe the fall of the Roman Empire, or the fall of the current world governments. Another symbolic view is this is not a world wide earth quake, but rather the destruction of the present world order. The political, social, and ecclesiastical will be reduced to chaos; This will be a breaking down of all authority, and the breaking up of all established and apparently permanent institutions.

The seals are self-contained series, culminating in this ultimate judgment at Christ's eschatological coming in glory. There are additional cycles to come. We have the trumpets and the bowl which will bring the same climax in their respective turns. One commentator writes, "We may set unhesitatingly set down as wrong all interpretations which view as the fulfillment of this passage any period except that of the Second Coming of Christ."

Let give my view here among the great thinkers. If we build upon my theory about the falling stars then these falling stars are the fallen ones who are just hanging around in the above heavens waiting for the judgment of Christ. They are waiting for the culmination of the ages. Is this outlandish? In view of all other theorist, of course it is. But let's understand one thing. The way things are on earth is the way things are in heaven as far as a structured society. On this earth we have those prisoners that are released on their own recognizance and they are waiting either trial, or just to be sentenced or just on probation. But one thing they all have in common and that is waiting for their judgment to either come to pass or their probation comes to an end. I think this theory is valid. Perhaps this is what is going on. Ancient writings indicate that at the 2012 date we will be returning to the time when we will have the return of the gods. If this is correct, and I say why not, then this has got to be what this passage is telling us. These could be the UFO's.

Like I said in the above pages, there is the undecipherable prophecies then there is reality. Prophecies are mostly interpretations of the scholars. They are all good ones too. But the reality paints s different picture. In the Christian community, most don't believe in UFO's. But the Bible differs on this point.

> **Acts 10:10,11,12 Says: {And he became hungry, and was desiring to eat; but while they were making preparations, he fell into a trance; * and he beheld the sky (heaven) opened up, and a certain object (vessel) like a great sheet coming down, lowered by four corners to the ground, * and there were all kinds of four footed animals and crawling (reptiles) creatures of the earth and birds of the air.}**

Now what does this say to you? Is this a UFO or what? This is a UFO now. Now that we have established UFO's using Scripture. This opens up a whole new view of possibilities here especially in the last days. Will there be aliens coming back here to earth in the later times? Well, if I was in my political right mind I would say hell no, are you kidding? There are no other living beings out there and if there was why would God allow them to visit a lawless planet? This has been my view for many years until the age of science fiction. Then I came across the above scripture. My view has change dramatically lately. So now that I am a lunatic and no longer in my right mind and just not politically correct then I will have to do an about face on this subject. I now can say yes there will be aliens coming back to earth. They are coming back very soon and Revelation tells us the same thing.

So we have two opposing views here. These falling stars could mean Intercontinental Ballistic Missiles. They could be asteroids. They could also be the falling angels returning to earth to do what God has commanded them to do. All makes sense. The Bible also states that when Satan fell from the heavens it looked like a bolt of lightening. The stars falling could be angelic beings just taking their time and going under the speed limit. But when they hit pay dirt they will hit with a thud. They are really in no hurry to get here. In Science fiction movies the sky is rolled back when a UFO comes out of hyperspace. After all they don't float around in the atmosphere, now do they? These ancients have been flying these things for eternity. Civilizations have been recording their presence since the beginning of time. This is like forever. In the above Scripture this is what has happened. The sky is rolled back and out comes a UFO. Somebody tell me this isn't so.

When they do land what ever it or they are they will land with a heavy thud. This tells me this is only a loud thud and not an explosion. More like a sonic boom. So they are not exploding what ever it is. There will also be lots of them. Then in verse 14 states then the sky was split apart. This tells me that the extraterrestrials will be coming as them selves and then they will come in their rides. In other words they will be flying in and walking.

When they arrive everybody in the Middle East will be heading for their caves in the mountains. Whatever happens or who ever this is that is arriving will scare the living shit out of the whole world, especially in the Middle East. We don't have too many caves in this world to house billions of human people. This passage of Scripture could only pertain to those who are in the Middle East.

In verse 15 it says that all the greatest people of the world will be scared shitless and are afraid for their lives. Their cities will not be safe for them. So they will run to the wilderness and hide under rocks. Sounds like the movie "Independence Day." They will also say "may the mountains fall on us and hide us from the one who sits on the throne." So what ever is happening here is telling them that these great angelic beings are God's messengers to earth and they are here to do God's judgment. Therefore people are afraid of "The one who sits on the throne". This is an angelic and demonic time. Humans will be getting a taste of other created beings and their awesome powers. This is only the beginning of things. This makes more sense as we get further along into the trumpet judgments when hell is unleashed, because this is the beginning right here. In verse 17 it says just that the great day of His wrath has come. It comes with the arrival of angelic and intelligent beings that have come out of eternity to visit man once again. This is the day when earth and the heavens meet. So in essence God is using the Extraterrestrials to bring judgment to all humanity.

What this symbolizes is the universality of the disasters. The question of whether the earthquake, the darkened sun, and so on, is to be taken literally or metaphorically, misses the point. That day will spell the end of the entire universe as we know it. Along with the end of the planets and the galaxies as well as the end of human institutions they may symbolize. Essentially it is the end of the ages.

> **Rev.8:1, 2 Says: {And when He broke the seventh seal, there was silence in heaven for about half an hour.* And I saw the seven angels who stand before God; and seven trumpets were given to them.}**

The seventh seal is not a judgment of it self but is the introduction of the trumpet judgments. Contained in the seventh seal are all the subsequent developments leading to the Second Coming of Christ, including the seven trumpets and the seven bowls of the wrath of God. The silence maybe compared to the silence of a foreman jurist who is about to report a verdict. For a moment there is perfect silence and everyone waits what will follow the announcement.

The brief silence in heaven contrast sharply with the noise and praise and song that characterized the heavenly scene in chapters 4 and 5.

With the opening of this last seal the book is now fully opened, and one would expect a holocaust to occur. Instead there is silence. This is a silence of expectancy, for this is the last seal. It is also a silence or foreboding that proceeds' the onslaught of judgments. It lasts for half an hour. This means just that half an hour.

> **Rev. 4-7 The Seven Sealed Scroll**—The lamb and the scroll are introduced to the reader in the vision of chapters 4 and 5. In some respects, this opening vision is more attention grabbing than the events that follows. Although revealing as it is, the throne of God in heaven and His unusual attendants enthusiastically worshipping Him for His holiness and His creative and redemptive acts. Not until the 5th chapter is John's attention drawn to the scroll in the hand of God. The contents of which are concealed by seven seals.

A call goes forth throughout the universe for a champion to come and break the seals and open the scroll. Initially, none is found qualified to open the scroll, causing John great dejection. At the crucial moment, Christ appears, depicted as the slain lamb, and takes the scroll from the hand of

God on the throne. All the inhabitants of heaven rejoice because one has finally come who is worthy to break the seven seals and open the scroll.

Chapter 6 marks a major change in the action, as the lamb successively breaks the seven seals which had formerly prevented the opening the cryptic scroll. Wild and terrifying things begin to transpire, beginning with four ominous horseman, and do not let up until nearly the end of the book.

The four Christian loyalist that stick fast and remain loyal. To the gospel do not agree about the time frame or import of this dramatic vision. Even those within each individual camp often disagree with reference to the details of interpretation. Those of every persuasion are inclined to see the principal significance of this throne room vision as an affirmation that God is sovereign over all and that the events which follow are the direct results of His righteous decrees. Most also agree that this vision underscores the unique qualifications of Christ to judge the wicked, based upon his sacrificial death. There is a wide range of opinions. They are not necessarily divided along the lines of the four approaches about the exact identity of the scroll.

Leading historicists take it to represent the purposes and designs of God or simply, future events. Then some preterist it means it is the sentence of the judge being handed down for execution. But to others it is the document representing the New Covenant.

Futurist typically see the sealed scroll as the title deed to the earth, to be reclaimed by Jesus Christ in the final seven years of history.

Spiritual interpreters have alternately identified it as the redemptive plan of God or God's last will and testament.

Where the four differences divide the most sharply, of course is in the timing of the earthly events which result in the breaking of the seven seals.

Historicist spread the fulfillment of the prophecies of the whole book over the entire age of the church and connect this breaking of the seals with events occurring early in the history of the church. Some taking the breaking of the seals back as far as the fall of Jerusalem in A D 70. On this view, the breaking of the seven seals concerns judgment of the Jewish commonwealth in the late sixties A.D. This is culminating in the doom of Jerusalem in A.D. 70. The more characteristics view among the historicist is the breaking of the first seal with the death of Domitian A.D. 96 and identifies the breaking of the other seals with events marking the rise of the Western Roman Empire and its degeneration, extending to the invasions of the Goths and vandals in the fourth and fifth centuries. The 144,000 sealed saints are the spiritual Israel (the church), preserved by God through these political upheavals.

Early date preterist agree with those historicist who see seal breaking as fulfilled in the fall of Jerusalem. They point out the unmistakable similarities between the images used here and those of the Olivet Discourse. This is in Mark 13 and Matt. 24 also in Luke 21:5, in which Jesus predicted the destruction of Jerusalem and the temple. The 144,000 represent the Judean Christians, who fled from Jerusalem prior to the siege and thus escaped the holocaust.

Futurist see in these chapters the beginning of the end-time tribulation. The four horsemen represent the Antichrist, followed by global calamities in the form of war, famine, and death. The 144,000 are Jews converted during the Tribulation. Dispensationalist believe that the church will already have been raptured, so these Jewish believers are a part of Israel, not the church.

Spiritualist interpreters do not look for specific single fulfillments of the visions in Revelation. The four horsemen depict the recurring historic phenomena of conquest, war, famine, and death without reference to any particular cases. Alternatively, the first horseman might depict Christ's gospel riding triumphantly through the earth. The point is that such events are sent into the world at the command of God and function as a part of His redemptive and retributive plan.

The martyrs seen in heaven remind those in every age who have suffered for Christ will be vindicated, and the 144,000 represent the church throughout history. Though the four approaches do not fully agree upon every detail of interpretation, there is not radical disagreement about the issues depicted in the opening throne room vision in chapter 4. Differences of general approach, however, begin to emerge in chapter 5 and become more conspicuous in chapter 6.

APOCALYPSE
SEVEN TRUMPET JUDGMENTS

Time frame: The trumpet judgments are connected to the two witnesses. We can see that by the "woes" mentioned in connection with the trumpet judgments at the end of the fifth trumpet judgment, it is announced: "One woe is past. Behold still two more woes are coming after these things." After the sixth trumpet judgment is described, and immediately following the presentation of the ministry, death, and the resurrection and then the ascension of the two witnesses the proclamation is given: "The second woe is past. Behold, the third woe is coming quickly." This means that the "woes" are attached to the ministry of the two witnesses is also attached to the trumpet judgments. In fact, the trumpet judgments are likely the very plagues that the two witnesses bring upon the world during their time here. The connection of the two witnesses shows us that the trumpet judgments take place during the first half of Daniels seventieth week, the first 1,260 days of the tribulation period.

Again there are these differences of opinions. These differences will continue till the end of this transcript.

Historicist approach The trumpets speak of a series of invasions against the Roman Empire. The Vandals, Huns, Saracens, and the Turks. The sixth trumpet brings the fall of Constantinople to the Turks in 1453. The little book represents the Bible being made available to the masses of Europe after the invention of the printing press.

Preterist Approach The first four trumpets correspond to disasters inflicted by the Romans on the Jews in the Jewish year of 66-70 A.D. The fifth trumpet probably depicts the demonic spirits rendering the besieged Jews irrational and self destructive. The sixth trumpet refers to Roman armies, who destroyed Jerusalem and slaughtered or deported all the Jews.

Futurist Approach Either literally of symbolically, the trumpets represent calamities that will be endured by the unrepentant inhabitants of the earth during the coming seven year tribulation. These may be supernatural judgments direct from the hand of God or merely the disastrous effects of man's improper stewardship of the death of the earth and his abuse of technology (Nuclear weapons).

Spiritual Approach Catastrophes reminiscent of the plagues of Egypt befall sinful humanity many times in history, demonstrating god's displeasure and, like trumpet blasts, warning of worse things to come upon the unrepentant. Sinful humanity typically absorbs these injuries with defiance, refusing to repent.

ECOLOGICAL DEATH

> **Rev.8:6, 7 Says: {And the seven angels who had the seven trumpets prepared themselves to sound them. * And the first sounded, and there came hail and fire, mixed with blood, and they were thrown to the earth; and a third of the earth was burned up, and all the green grass was burned up.}**

A third of the earth burned up could be the result of a nuclear war. Let me reiterate something here at this early stage of interpretation. These events could mostly mean that they take place in the Middle East. Why is this So? Well no place on earth is more important than this concentrated area. If you don't think so then just watch the daily news. But of course this is not written in stone. All of the earth will be affected as well. I wonder if the Middle East takes up one third of the earth.

Most interpreters identify this trumpet with the military conflicts between the Western Roman Empire and hordes of Goths and Vandals under Alaric. During these wars there was a tremendous sound of the gothic trumpets. Rome was so stunned because they have not had such invaders for the last eight hundred years. Rome evacuated Britain to reinforce its northern borders. The Goths attacked Gaul, Spain, and Italy from the north, burning and destroying everything in its path. Blood and great fire and the burning of trees and herbage marked their path. In the year 410 A.D. the city of Rome got sacked. Rome was besieged and split into one third, namely the western division. This was, at this time one third of the known world. On the other hand, there may be an actual reference to the destruction of actual vegetation in the land. Much of the beautiful foliage and trees around Jerusalem were destroyed by the Romans in the war.

With reference to the Egyptian plague, professionals have attempted naturalist explanations for this unique event in ancient Egypt. It could be attributed to discharges from an encroaching comet. Others have suggested the fire running along the ground was the rare phenomenon known as St Elmo's fire. This did involve existing natural phenomena such as hail, thunder and fire and rain. This was considered a special providential miracle. This includes special organizing of factors influencing natural phenomena, possibly through angelic agencies. The most modern explanation is that the catastrophes describe in this trumpet is the direct result of nuclear weapons being detonated. This grass that is burned up is not only grass but also all vegetation that is closely aligned with it. We have grass growing with oats, wheat, rice grains. These are the foods that are the staple of the world. Because of this connection comes massive erosion of soil comes continued floods and where there is floods there is mudslides, which we see periodically in the news. All the air will be polluted as well. This will throw all ecology into chaos and doom.

> **Rev.8:8, 9 Says: {And the second angel sounded, and something like a great mountain burning with fire was thrown into the sea; and a third of the sea became blood; * and a third of the creatures, which were in the sea and had life, died; and a third of the ships were destroyed.}**

From the historical perspective. This great mountain is the Vandals. King Genseric, known as the Tyrant of the sea, terrorized the Romans and sunk their ships for over one hundred years. For over six centuries no hostile ship had disputed Rome's mastery of the sea. The Vandals left their ancient home on the Baltic to invade Rome, destroying their ships and disrupting their commerce. These Vandals were the main cause of the downfall of the Roman Empire. As they ravaged the sea they also invaded Spain and Gaul and had their mariners slaughtered and pirated the seas for over thirty years. Portions of the sea became blood. Over the course the Goths and the Vandals sacked Rome time and again. This storm fell heavily upon the maritime cities and countries of the Roman Empire.

Another view is that if these are literal events, there is also a symbolic dimension to them. The symbol of the mountain like object falling into the sea probably symbolizes the influence of what is popularly called the revived Roman Empire. The sea is a symbol of the gentile nations and that the mountain falling into the sea suggests a time when the Antichrist led coalition will fall upon the Gentiles of the world like a flaming sword, destroying mountain. Conquering the Gentile nations and destroying many Gentile lives.

This is not a literal mountain. It is used figuratively in the words of Jesus in Matt. 21:21 when He stated that if you have faith as a mustard seed you may say to this mountain be cast into the sea. Another interesting analogy is found in Jeremiah 51:25. A mountain in Scripture language represents a kingdom. The sea is typical of nations, some kingdom internally on fire. This is hinting at revolution and will become a restless sea of nations. The result will be the greater destruction of life and commerce, which is represented by the ships.

Another view is the fact that a literal mountain hurling from space towards earth and impacts the sea and destroys all the ships and a third of the earth with it. This has got to be steered by the angelic host of heaven. This event seems the most likely explanation accessible at this time. Maybe a giant meteorite, or maybe a giant asteroid, or even a satellite orbiting one of the other planets, could be propelled towards earth by cosmic forces of which we have no knowledge yet.

Perhaps this huge asteroid just might be the planet Nibiru, also known as Lucifer hammer. Although its actual collision with the sea will be in only one impact location, it is evident that the entire world will know about it. People will observe it for some time approaching from space, then it will enter the earth's gravitational field and hurl itself to the earth at its precise location. To destroy a third of the world's ships it has got to land in the Mediterranean Sea. This location is where one third of the world's oil is coming from. It is the center of commerce of the world. Maybe not yet but it will be.

Think about this for a moment. What if a hydrogen bomb was to explode in the Mediterranean Sea? With all those oil ships going through there with oil and goods being imported and exported from the Middle East. This would be a catastrophe of Biblical proportions.

Jeremiah 51:24-30 Says: {"But I will repay Babylon and all the inhabitants of Chaldea for all their evil that they have done in Zion before my eyes." declares the Lord. * "Behold, I am against you, O destroying mountain who destroy the whole earth," declares the Lord, "And I will stretch out my

hand against you, And roll you down from the crags And I will make you a burnt out mountain, * "And they will not take from you even a stone for a corner Nor a stone for foundations, But you will be desolate forever," declares the Lord. * Lift up a signal (standard) in the land, Blow a trumpet among the nations! Consecrate the nations against her. Summon against her and Appoint a marshal against her, Bring up the horses like bristly locusts. * Consecrate the nations against her, The kings of the Medes, Their governors and all their prefects, And every land of their dominion.* So the land quakes and writhes, For the purposes of the Lord against Babylon stand, To make the land of Babylon without inhabitants.}

In these passages the word mountain is meant Babylon and their belief system. It is symbolic of the pride of man. God has a time period when he judge's her. But He has already done so in past history. To do so again in future history is expected again. He even is going to call up the horse locust from the abyss. He is also making a case against her in the minds of the world. If I am reading this right the inhabitants will one day be gone. Does this mean all of the inhabitants of the land? If so then the people of Iraq will be wiped off the map. This mountain will be like a burnt out mountain. Burnt out as like with fire. Consecrate means to devote to a solemn purpose, to declare sacred. This connotes a religious fervor. This is an emotional drive.

This mountain in the second trumpet is related. But then again maybe it isn't. I brought it into play because the Scriptures usually indicate one thing but in this case the word mountain probably means mountain literally. Which do we take it literally? Let's just say both are right. If the word mountain means Babylon and the word sea means nations, kingdoms. The above Scripture also declared God will pay them back for what they have done to Zion. Then this passage could be interpreted like this: The pride of man and their belief system that destroyed God's people and all of the nations and the kingdoms that were involved will be burnt up like a fire. They will go down the hard way. The past history indicates this to be the exact case. All of the nations rise and then fall on their own accord. As it was in the past so it will be in the future. The horse like locust will be let loose and they will bring this business to a close and they will be God's avengers. It will be done with religious fervor. It has been decreed by Jehovah Himself, destroying a third of the ships in the process. Now Babylon is located right next to the Mediterranean Sea. Ships are symbolic of commerce and economic welfare.

> **Rev.8:10, 11 Says: {And the third angel sounded, and a great star fell from heaven, burning like a torch, and it fell on a third of the rivers and on the springs of waters: * and the name of the star is called wormwood; and a third of the waters became wormwood; and many men died from the waters, because they were made bitter.}**

I heard it said that the word wormwood in Ukraine means Chernobyl. Chernobyl was a nuclear reactor that melted down in Russia sometime back. This star is associated with sulfur.

Back to the historical perspective; The great star of the vision is Attila the Hun. He was called the "scourge of God." The Romans new very little about the Huns. They suddenly arrived on the scene like a blazing meteor. Attila assembled 800,000 men upon the banks of the Danube. As the Vandals were masters of the sea then the Huns were masters of the rivers. They decimated this region. They shed so much blood in the Italian Alps that over 300,000 men were slaughtered and this even polluted the waters of the springs there. Many men died drinking the waters and still continue to die those who drink the waters, through famine and pestilence and disease. If this star was a meteorite then this one star has only one impact. To poison the worlds water ways we would have to have a lot more of these impacts of meteors. One is just not enough. Maybe this could mean a giant set of meteors divinely visiting the earth. This must be the conditions necessary to fulfill the prophecy. Therefore this theory is speculation as all have been.

In the Old Testament, the name of the fallen star is called wormwood, a term used in the Law of the Prophets to warn Israel of its destruction as a punishment for their apostasy. Again by combining these Old Testament allusions, St John makes this point: Israel is apostate, and has become an Egypt; Jerusalem has become a Babylon; and the covenant breakers will be destroyed, as surely as Egypt and Babylon were destroyed.

If the meaning is symbolic, there is no clear indication as to the interpretation of this judgment except that the great star can be assigned to some personage such as the Antichrist or Satan himself and the waters could be regarded as symbolic of the peoples of the earth. It seems preferable, however, to see this with a reasonable literalness, as in the case of the second trumpet. The star seems to be a heavenly body or a mass from outer space, understandably burning as it enters the atmosphere of the earth, falling with contaminating influence upon the earth's waters and peoples.

Another possible view is that it may pertain to our belief system of the earth, mainly the apostate religious fervor during the tribulation. Let's examine the person known as the Pope. The Pope will be a main attraction during these times. The Pope will be associated with the antichrist. This will be known as the papal religious system. This could be the falling star. This would mean that this falling star is some person who claimed authority and who becomes apostate, whose fall produces the awful results given here. It may be the final Antichrist who first may have claimed to be for Israel a great teacher with divine authority and then takes the awful plunge. Wormwood is his name and the waters became wormwood and bitter. It stands for great corruption.

Stars in prophetic scriptures are religious dignitaries. "They that turn many to righteousness are to shine like stars forever." Here we have a star whose influence over man is so great that when he falls the third part of men are poisoned because of the evil influence of this apostate leader. Who is this star? Let me give you a hint. Who is the most apostate Christian on the planet? The answer is that he is the most popular Christian on the planet, the Pope. The Pope occupies the highest place in the church in the minds of billions of people world wide. Many would say, who else? Now think for a moment what might be the effect on billions of people if tomorrow the news reported that the Pope declares that all Christianity was a sham, a fraud, a joke, not really real, that Christianity was all illusional and the result of the mystical mind. God is not really real. It is said that Pope Leo X did this privately. What do you think the response will be when he does this openly to the whole world? I think what this says is that a retarded great and strong spirit will be cast down like all the rest of the retarded spirits and his arrival will be deadly. He will poison the minds of those who are apostate. A third of these people who are in some belief system will become as dead men as a result of drinking this belief system. Behind all diseases are spirits.

Behind all things are spirits. Catch the spirit is to catch the belief system behind it, then the doing of it with your energy. It is through you that the spirit of the thing moves into this material plane, because you were moved by the spirit. This is how evil and good enters this earth. So it just stands to reason that spirits are behind all things. As mentioned above millions of stars will be falling back to earth at this time because they are all waiting judgment. There are those who are in the heavens above then there are those who are in the earth below. There are also those who are in deeper trouble with God and he has them locked up a little closer to Him. Those who occupy the above heavens are on their own recognizance. They are not locked up. They will return when the time is ripe. In modern times we have been visited by these U F O's already. Get ready for the earth's vibrations will start changing soon. This is your sign.

> **Rev. 8:12 Says: {And the fourth angel sounded, and a third of the sun and a third of the moon and a third of the stars were smitten, so that a third of them might be darkened and the day might not shine for a third of it, and the night in the same way. }**

The view from history is the sun, the moon, and the stars represent the political firmament of the Roman Empire. The conquest of Rome and the end of its imperial rule was accomplished by Heruli under the command of Odoacer in the year of 476 A.D. Romulus-Augustus was banished. So was his office. The darkening of the heaven luminaries is everywhere an emblem of any great calamity. It is not to be a total destruction though. It is not as if the moon and the sun and stars were totally blotted out entirely. For there was still some remaining light. For a third part of the day and a third part of the night, this darkness reigned. This does not imply that there will be light again? There can be no difficulty applying this to Odoacer and to his reign. This is a time when the Roman's came to an end.

Another view is that this event could very well be the outcome of a nuclear blast, better yet a thermonuclear blast. There will be exchanges of these atomic weapons during this time. When this happens one third of the light and one third of the dark is a reduction of these sources that results from the air being polluted. There will be tremendous air pollution left from the nuclear blast.

The sun is the symbol of the highest authority, the moon, who has not her own light, is symbolic of derived authority and the stars are symbolic of subordinate authority. The symbolical meaning of this trumpet judgment is that all authority within the revived Roman Empire will be smitten by the hand of God from above and as a result there will be the most awful moral darkness.

The darkness prefigures the gloom and doom of the ungodly and is also a prelude to the new exodus of God's people from under the oppressive hand of the current world rulers. In an age which looks to the stars for guidance, this verse reminds us that God exercises complete control over the solar system.

God can turn even the most benign influences of the sun and the moon as well as the planets into means for the destruction of man and the stupid human race. In the countless evils which have their origin in the excess or defect of the power of the sun, we may see an illustration of this judgment. All evil are due to the abnormal; functioning of the heavenly bodies throughout the entire ages. Therefore the entire universe, including the sun the moon and the stars are used by our Lord of the heavens as a warning for those who do not serve Him and are against those who prosecute His Children.

God has always put the prosecutors on the hot seat for messing with His elect. He uses time along with bad unforeseen circumstances. He Also whistles for calamity of those who are ungodly. Whistle is a vibration and a calling for the spirit of calamity.

Rev. 8:13 Says: {And I looked, and I heard an eagle (one eagle) flying in mid-heaven, saying with a loud voice, "Woe, woe, woe, to those who dwell on the earth, because of the remaining blasts of the trumpet of the three angels who are about to sound!"}

In the view of the past, this angel is pronouncing a turning point. The Western Roman Empire has been destroyed in the Gothic period described under emblems of the first four trumpets. The final three trumpets, each referred to as a woe, turn our attention to the eastern Roman Empire and its destruction. After that, the prophecy will turn our view back to the West, where Rome will be seen again in a new form.

The final trumpets are designated as woes because of the surpassing intensity and duration of the judgments. The first woe is the Saracens' conquest Southern and the Eastern third empire; the second woe is the Turkish conquest of the remaining third of the east; and the third woe is the judgments of the seven bowls, which will be poured out upon the papacy. This has been identified with the French revolution and its results.

Another view is that this is referring to the days after Jesus. These woes are supposed by many learned men to refer to the destruction of Jerusalem;

the first woe is the seditions among the Jews themselves; the second woe is the besieging of the city by the Romans; and the third woe is the taking and the sacking of the city, and the burning of the Temple. This was the greatest of all the woes, as in it the city Temple were destroyed and nearly one million men lost their lives.

As terrible as the last trumpets were the next will be much worse. The first four judgments on the earth are physical in characteristics. The last fours trumpets are not just judgments of themselves but also serve as warnings of the next three judgments which will be far worse and severe in character.

They are all divine warnings to demonic woes. This is a preview of the ultimate judgment of the unrepentant man to the punishment reserved for the devil and his fallen ones.

As the first four seals, with their horsemen were set off from the last three, so the first four trumpets are set apart from the last three by this heavenly announcement that the latter will be more ominous than the former. This suggests that the calamities which occur throughout history will become more intense as the end approaches.

THE BOTTOMLES PIT

Rev.9:1-12 Says: {And the fifth angel sounded, and I saw a star from heaven which had fallen to the earth; and the key to the bottomless pit (shaft of the abyss) was given to him. * And he opened the bottomless pit; and smoke went up out of the pit, like the smoke of a great furnace; and the sun and the air were darkened by the smoke of the pit. * And out of the smoke came forth locusts upon (into) the earth; and power was given them, as the scorpions of the earth have power. * And they were told that they should not hurt the grass of the earth, nor any green thing, nor any tree, but only the men who did not have the seal of God on their foreheads. * And they (it was given to them) were not permitted to kill anyone, but to torment for five months; and their torment was like the torment of a scorpion when it stings a man. * And in those days men shall seek death and will not find it; and they will long to die and death flees from them.* And the appearance of the locust (appearances) of the locusts was

like horses prepared for battle; and on their heads, as it were, crowns like gold, and their faces were like the faces of men. * And they had hair like the hair of a woman, and their teeth were like the teeth of lions.* and they had breastplates like breastplates of iron; and the sound of their wings was like the sound of many chariots, of many horses rushing into battle. * And they have tails like scorpions, and stings; and in their tails is their power to hurt men for five months. * They have as king over them, the angel of the abyss; his name in Hebrew is Abadon (destruction), and in the Greek he has the name Apollyon (destroyer). * The first woe is past; behold two woes are still coming after these things.}

In view of the past history, the locust represents the Saracens (Muslim Arabs) and their campaigns against the Roman Empire from about 612 to 763 A.D. The king that is over them is Mohammed. The star fallen from heaven is a symbol for a prince who has been degraded and deprived of his rank. Mohammed was of princely pedigree, but the previous generation of his family had lost rule. In addition to this in Biblical times the locust often came from Arabia. These are the actual; locust plagues. It is suggested that the word locust mean the same thing as Arab to the Jewish nation. The names of the one and of the other being in similar pronouncements is Locust (arbeth) and of an Arab (arbi).

Mohammeds instruction to the Koran is similar to the words here as not to harm the green things of the earth. Mohammeds instructions were to "Destroy no palm trees, nor any fields of corn, nor to cut down any of the fruit trees," This policy was in stark contrast to the slash and burn practices of the Gothic invaders. The Saracens (Arabs) were not able to kill Papal Rome as a political body, but they did terrorize it for a while. So in the meantime they laid waste the Greek and the Latin churches, they could not annihilate these political parties. But they sacked them pretty hard. The phrase "who do not have the seal on their foreheads." This is meaning their tormenters. They targeted their tormenters assaults who were corrupt, idolatrous Christians against whom the Arabs did prevail.

As for "the five months" This is seen in the prophetic months of thirty days each. Thirty days is equivalent to thirty years which comes to thirty times five is one hundred fifty years. Mohammed adopted the policy of making converts by the sword in the year 612 A.D. This is the time the Arabs began to attack the eastern churches and seek to force new converts of European descendants from Christianity to Islam. They ravaged and pillaged until they were stopped in the year 732 A.D. In the following years about 763 A.D. they had stopped their aggression and moved their capital to Baghdad.

There is a remarkable parallelism between this scripture and these events.

This trumpet could be describing political or ecclesiastical events. The fallen star could be the third bishop of Rome. Having forfeited the keys of heaven he now has the keys to hell, to unleash damnable doctrines and deception upon the church, this damage is spiritual not physical. These demonic doctrines do not kill per say, but subject men to spiritual torment for a limited time which is five months.

At the same time the words fallen star is not literal. The personal pronoun is used here and is indication a deity. This is saying that a personality was represented by this star. It may be some angel or some religion or a high priest, or some religious teachers that spread unbelief, like heresies, false principles that wreck morality to the core. This tears down societies. This means that these locusts that came out of the bottomless pit were moral and spiritually decaying doctrines. This would explain why the chosen ones were unaffected. The fact that there is decaying moral doctrine in our world is not surprising to say the least. In fact it is an understatement. For the sanity and civility our civilizations will vanish altogether. Any one who is a Christian can see that possibility of a massive demonic delusion will account for the behavior of our modern world. We are currently becoming demonized. In the future we will be entirely demonized. The apparent national insanity is already apparent as one can listen to the news and read the headlines daily. There are those who have lost all ability to reason. There are the frenzied mobs attacking one another in the Middle East and other locations around the world. There are the deluded multitudes following the most transparent false prophets, and the crazy and the desperate chase after food. There are also the mass murders, the executions and the suicides and the fathers slaughtering their own families and the mothers eating their own children. Satan and his cronies Swarm through the earth and swallow it up. Things will not get better.

The "Key to the bottomless pit" however could represent a system of teaching and the development of apostasy with it. The kind of apostasy that is associated with the Pope because he is the head of the world church. We are not far off the mark or wrong if we identify with this coming delusion with the occult system of Gnostic origin, the ones that are so largely prevailing in modern times and is rapidly spreading as we speak. Listed here are a few but not limited to are the New thought, New Theology, Eddyism (Christian Science), Spiritism, theosophy and other offshoots. The locust is now interpreted as the spiritual plague of the last days.

Many in the Christian community believe that this star falling is a deity, possibly Satan himself with the keys of the abyss. After all he is there chief executive officer. The reason is this: Sometimes the word "star" refers to a heavenly body. But this word is often used to refer to some kind of intelligent creature like a deity. Both meanings are right. After all this is where we get the phrase "That girl was a star." We use it as a figure of speech. The bottomless pit is the prison house of demons. Therefore, we can conclude the locust as demonic hordes will be released against the unrepentant humanity during the tribulation period.

As Satan unlocks the prison house of the fallen angels and the most awful satanic agencies come forth to begin their awful work of torment. The smoke is symbolizing the darkening of the minds of the world order. The locust next is symbolic of demon powers and those who come under their spell. All the apostates like Israel and the apostate Christians will suffer greatly. All things religious will be doomed. The light of the gospel is now completely blotted out like the sun. The darkness coming from the pit is symbolic of the demonic powers coming forth. Demon possession and their works will become the norm.

Evil will cloud all men's minds and darkens their understandings. These demons will be robbing humanity of all light that is of all true righteousness and holiness, joy and peace. This judgment will cause torment because they will realize they are the ones doomed to hell for all eternity. That is why death will not find them. In a big way death it is finding them. Death is in their face already. They will be completely devoid of all understanding of the light of truth which directs men's lives and guides us in the right way giving us peace to the soul. Their vision will become darkened by the deceptions and the delusions set loose by the devil himself. All of hells lies will be unleashed upon the earth. All of humanity will be tortured like those who are in the abyss. The statement "men will desire to die, and death will flee from them" is interpreted as meaning: As is the manner in demonic affliction as recorded in the gospels, "those caught in the grip of demon possession are not free to exercise their own will" therefore they are not free to take their own lives. By going one step further the effect of this drive is to drive humanity to suicide but they will be unable to die. There will be no death at this time. After all where are they going to go to hell? The prison gates have been unlocked. There is no going to hell. All of hell has been transferred to the earthly plain. Earth is the meeting place. All heavenly bodies descend. All demonic hell spirits ascend and they will be flying cobra helicopters and spraying nerve gas from their tails all over the earth. All of the fallen creation will meet on the earthly plain for their judgments. Christ is on His way.

The locust is a very fitting symbol for the Islamic hordes. Arab hordes are likened as to their numbers, to locust invading. Islamic tradition speaks of locusts having dropping into the hands of Mohammed. Bearing on their wings the words "We are the army of the great God." Their turbans can be seen as a crown. And the hair like women and the faces like men are seen in reference to their bearded and long haired heads. The breastplates were literal. The Saracens had iron coats of mail. The Koran states: "God has given you coats of mail to defend you in your wars." The sting in their tails may well refer to the fact that the Saracens were known to be adept at fighting rearward over the tails of their horses.

But others believe the locust also mentioned here is thought to mean the demons that were let loose on besieged city of Jerusalem as a judgment against those who had rejected Christ.

Though the demons themselves are no doubt a portrayal of armies of demons that afflicted the whole society of the Jews during the conflicts with the Romans, the demonized zealots that made life miserable for the Jews at this time may actually be in reference to the transvestites. They had hair as women and faces as men. This is insane thinking I know.

"With their insatiable hunger for loot, they ransacked the houses of the wealthy, murdered the men and violated women for sport; they drank their spoils with blood, and from mere society and shamelessness gave themselves up to effeminate practices, plaiting their hair and putting on women's clothes, drenched themselves with perfumes and painting their eyelids to make themselves attractive. They copied not merely the dress, but also the passions of women, devising in their excess of licentiousness unlawful pleasures in which they wallowed as in a brothel. Thus they entirely polluted the city with their foul practices. Yet they wore women's faces, their hands were murderous. They would approach with mincing steps, suddenly they become fighting men, and, whipping out their dyed cloaks, they would run through every passer by". Jesus did say that the Jewish apostates were children of the devil and a synagogue of Satan.

Israel's conquerors always came from Assyria, Babylon, Medo-Persia. The 10th legion Roman army was stationed at the Euphrates at this time.

The invasion of Jerusalem during this time was scheduled so precisely for the hour and the day and the month and the year. This was a predestined event. The destruction of Jerusalem was one of the prophesied events that carried a clear time designation. Daniels famous prophecy of the seventy weeks predicts that the people of the prince who is to come shall destroy the city and the sanctuary. The end of it shall be with a flood of armies, and until the end of the war desolations are determined. These things are said to occur at a specific time connected with the seventy weeks.

The same goes for the end of days in modern times. The destruction of Jerusalem will come when you see armies surround the city of Jerusalem then you will know that its desolation is near. Jesus said assuredly that this generation will not pass away till all of these things are fulfilled. Jesus also hinted that the destruction of Jerusalem was the ultimate theme of all Old Testament prophecy. For these are the days of vengeance, that all things that are written may be fulfilled.

Another view is that new age heresies under the leadership of a future apostate Pope. These symbols here intermingle, all of which are very evidently found in the occult systems to which we have referred. Faces as of men would seem to imply intelligence, and these teachers make a great appeal to human reason, while they themselves follow illogical theories. They are characterized by seductiveness and attractive fancies typified by the hair of women. The iron breastplate refers to utter destruction of conscience to those who believe in them. These heresies render them impervious to the shafts of truth.

The locust king if not Satan himself then it is a high ranking subordinate. Since the name is given in both Greek and Hebrew suggests that his power will be over both Jews and the Gentiles.

Either way you look at it, the faces of men means that they, the demons are intelligent. The hair like women means they can be seductive. Their teeth like lions; teeth, means they speak with ferocity. They are like scorpions mean they are malicious. Their breastplates of iron means they are appearing invulnerability and are war like. They cannot be resisted by humanly means. This shows us that a plague in which devastation, malice, kinglike authority; intelligence, seductiveness, fierceness, strength, meet together under one directing spirit, to torment men.

ARMY FROM THE EAST

> **Rev. 9:13-21 Says: {And the sixth angel sounded, and I heard (one voice) a voice from the four horns of the golden alter which is before God. * one saying to the sixth angel who had the trumpet, "Release the four angels who are bound at the great river Euphrates." * And the four angels, who had been prepared for the hour and day and month and year, were released, so that they might kill a third of mankind. * And the number of the armies of the horsemen was two hundred million; I heard the number of them. * And this is how I saw in the vision of the horses and those who sat on them: the riders had breastplates the color of fire and of hyascinth and of brimstone: and the heads of the horses are like the heads of lions; and out of their mouths proceed fire and smoke and brimstone (sulfur). * A third of mankind was killed by these three plagues, by the fire and the smoke and the brimstone (sulfur), which proceeded out of their mouths. * For the power of the horses are in their mouths and in their tails; for their tails are like serpents and have heads; and with them they do harm. * And the rest of mankind, who were not killed by these plagues, did not repent of the works of their hands, so as not to worship demons, and the idols of gold and of silver and of brass and of stone and of wood, which can neither see nor hear or walk; * and they did not repent of their murders nor of their sorceries nor of their immorality nor of their thefts.}**

The third of mankind upon whom this woe falls in the eastern third, or Grecian portion of what had been the Roman Empire. This was the Byzantine Empire, with its capital in Constantinople. Right before the year 1000 A.D, a fierce and numerous people known as the Tartars moved from the area of the Caspian Sea to new settlements on the eastern banks of the Euphrates. Under the leadership of Togrul, the Turkomans, as they came to be called, established a formidable empire in western Asia. The Turkomans conquered Baghdad, the capital of the Saracen Empire, in 1055, and converted to the Islamic religion, Persia and India also being subjugated. It would have seemed natural for the Turks to expand west across the Euphrates. Yet for a long time they had now been inactive, and it would seem they had been bound or restrained by some mighty power from moving in their conquest to the West. The Turks finally crossed the Euphrates and made assaults upon the Byzantine Empire.

The Turkish Empire in those days was divided into four principalities under Shahs four sons. Almost four hundred years later, in 1453 the Turks by this time known as the Ottomans empire conquered Constantinople, bringing it to an end the last vestige of the Roman Empire in the east. The Turkish hordes are the horsemen described in this vision. The increments of time: an hour, and a day, and a month, and the year are to be added together. Calculating by the year for the day method, an hour is either one twelfth or one twenty fourth of a year; a day is a year, a month is 30 years; and a year is either 360 or 365 years, depending upon whose calendar is followed.

The four angels bound at the Euphrates River are the four Sultans bordering on that river, where they are confined till after the period of the Crusades.

The term two hundred million can be interpreted as "two myriad myriads." This can be transmuted to mean an indefinite number. The term myriad was used to describe the myriads of Turkish horsemen spreading over the Greek frontier.

From their appearance the Ottomans have affected to wear warlike apparel of scarlet, blue, and yellow.

The fire, smoke and the brimstone is a reference to the artillery, for these great guns were first used by the Turks at the siege of Constantinople. The armies under Sultan Mahomet were armed with 67 cannons. The smallest fired a stone shot weighing 200 pounds. The largest with a bore of three feet could hurl a 1,200 pound ball.

The reference to the power in their tails means that there was a general that did not know how to rally his troops so he cut off a horse's tail and fixed it to the end of a spear. The soldiers seeing it would rally to a point, gaining the victory.

The second view is a figurative view in that this vision refers to the Roman armies and their confederates, following upon the demonic "locust" Invasions that came upon the apostates of Israel. Many of the troops that came into Palestine were previously stationed at the Euphrates River. The river was the boundary between Israel and her ancient captors. It was across the Euphrates that Assyria came and carried Israel into captivity. And it was across the Euphrates that Babylon came and carried Judah into captivity.

The great conquerors of Palestine and Egypt had come across the Euphrates in ancient times.

This invasion was scheduled so precisely for the hour and the day and the month and the year. In short it was a predestined event. The destruction of Jerusalem was one of the prophesied events that carried a clear time designation, spoken of by the prophet Daniel famous prophet of the seventy weeks. The people of the prince who is to come shall destroy the city and the sanctuary.

The army is fearsome in appearance and in numbers, although the number given is two hundred million is not to be taken literally. It is not for certain whom this great army represented. The confederates of Rome came from the east and assisted Rome in this Jewish war or whether it has a general reference to the Roman armies only. Two hundred million horsemen would have been impossible but these numbers are impressive enough and was without a doubt meant for impression only. But one thing is for sure is that this army is the fulfillment of all the warnings in the law and the prophets of an avenging horde are sent to punish the Covenant-breakers. In Duet.28 Moses warned Israel that violating their covenant with Jehovah would bring great curse upon them. The final curse would be an overwhelming and devastating invasion of foreign armies, who would drive them out of their homeland and send them throughout the world.

The trumpet is referred to the end of this besieging of the city of Jerusalem when the Romans punched through the wall and swarmed into the city. It may refer to the initial invasion of the Romans in 66 A.D. The first view is more preferable as the end of a section dealing with Israel, and God is now dealing with Rome in judgment.

The next view is divided into two camps. These bizarre horsemen are either demonic spirits or they are literal armies described in figurative terms. If they are the second then they will refer to the Orient. This army might be composed of human beings and then maybe it won't. It might equally be an army of demons. The language seems to mingle the elements of the human and the demonic, the natural and the supernatural. In this way it is impossible to tell the difference. There are examples in Scriptures where we have the same thing. 2 Kings 2:11 and 6:13-17. Also in Rev.19:14. But the weapons of this army have weapons of hell and may further indicate that the army is made up of the inhabitants of hell.

Since the locust of the previous trumpets is seen as demonic hosts, one should wonder why we have the same two descriptions of the same phenomenon. Now if they are human armies then this number is two hundred million then we have a big problem. It is virtually impossibly for one nation or even one coalition to have more than one million wearing the uniform during a conflict. The combined troops of the United Nations is about one million. The former Soviet Union was the largest in the world but they had only 3.2 million. China did have 2.3 million. This is in retrospect though. For there to be two hundred million then all of the armies of the world have to be involved here.

It is believed by many that what John sees in his visions is the machinery of modern or future military destruction translated into the military terminology of his day. The identification of the individual features of his visions is such apparatus as tanks, rockets, jets, and troop carriers along with helicopter gun ships.

"The breastplates of fiery red, hyacinth blue, and sulfur yellow refers to the modern warfare under way. The horses that have heads of lions, and out of their mouths came fire, smoke, and brimstone" refers to the modern mechanical warfare. "Their tails are like serpents, having heads; and with them they do harm" is referring to being symbols or are the best description John can give of modern warfare. This is an awesome picture of an almost irresistible military force destroying all that opposes it. This is also a picture of thermonuclear warfare. Smoke represents the immense clouds of radioactive fallout and debris. The brimstone is melted earth along with our building materials. The nationality of this army is not clear. This army is human and not a countless multitude of evil spirits, as some wonder. This great army could be the imperial army of the antichrist. This army could consist of Mohammedans. This vision specifically belongs to the time of the end.

The vision of John does not mention who is being attacked. The land of Israel is nearest and will suffer the most. The revived Roman Empire will be the objective of the invading hordes. The revived Roman Empire is the coming European Confederacy.

If the Mohammedans are under the leadership of the antichrist they will come against the revived Roman Empire. To destroy the Islamic confederacy there has to be a declaration of war. This is what I will call the Clash of the Titans. In this view of things it would make sense to say that doesn't have to make sense.

Now fast forward to modern day armies. Today it is possible for the nation of China to field two hundred million soldiers alone. Consider the billions of people in the Orient today. A literal army of two hundred million of horses is unimaginable. The main idea in this message is that a vast and overwhelming army that is beyond comprehension and is exceeding far beyond anything ever witnessed in the history of the earth.

It is not necessary to limit the nature of this trumpet to the invasion of either Rome or Israel. According to the more widespread view the vision depicts often recurring phenomena. Many feel the afflictions portrayed here are spiritual in nature. The spiritual evils which afflict the ungodly in this life and the number of the inflictions is indeed great enough to be described as "two myriads of myriads." They destroy a part but not the greater part of men or the earth. Such punishment is a foretaste of hell, as seems to be foreshadowed in the fire and smoke and brimstone of verses 17 and 18.

The aim of this plague is to exhibit the death-working power of false thoughts, false customs, and false beliefs, and to rouse humanity to forsake all false worship, worldliness and self indulgence into which we have all have fallen.

The two hundred million is not to be taken literally any more than the other features of the vision. An actual army of this vastness would form a column one mile wide and eighty miles long.

The horse's tails are thought to represent the after math of war. The serpents-poison after wars end is never completely eradicated. It always continues to bear its evil influence. Rather than representing a single conflict at the end of the age this battle with its two hundred million horsemen can apply instead to all the wars at all times throughout this dispensation.

The death dealing horsemen of the sixth trumpet are not tanks and planes. Better yet they are not only tanks and planes. They are also cancers and diseases and the terrorist bombs. A lot of things are really not clear but one thing is. The general idea of these trumpets is that throughout the entire period, extending from the first to the second coming of Christ will again and again punish the prosecutors of the church by inflicting upon them disasters in every sphere of life.

Have we not twice in the year 1919-1918 and again in the year 1939-1945 seen the bottomless pit open and the hells of war unleashed? The heavens have been darkened by swarms of evil things that came from it? Has not the thunder of two hundred million hellish horsemen shaken the earth in our own day?

During these times there will be no repentance. The reasons are many. From false doctrines to the drugs, the specific sins to the papal early time period was immorality, idolatry, murders and sorceries along with thefts.

Today it is the same. The unbelievers' lack of repentance at this time is truly astonishing. With half of the world dead by the plagues and war, and with the disruption of the ecosystem and economy and the weather pattern in chaos one would expect that these survivors who witnessed these calamities would repent. But this will not be the case. Their hard hearts will be as iron. They will not be able to see the truth in any form. Their eyes are totally blinded by false truth. They will have believed delusions. In the futility of their mind, having understood darkened beliefs, they are being alienated from the life of God because of the ignorance that is in them. The blindness is in their hearts who are being past feeling, having given themselves over to lewdness, to work all uncleanness with greediness.

The verses of 20 and 21 give us an inside view of the glimpse into the religious and moral conditions during the tribulation period. The religion of these times and the life of those unredeemed men upon the earth will be the worship of demons and idols. Humanity will be filled with murder, sorcery, and fornication and stealing. From the word sorcery we derive in English the pharmacy. Sorceries then must include the misuse of all drugs. The use and the mis-use of drugs are predominant in our western culture as well as around the world. Sorceries suggest the use of consciousness altering drugs. These illegal substances have defied the law enforcement agencies. They are taking society by storm through the psychiatric profession's drugs to mental patients. Theft always remains a problem, especially in the drug industry.

CHRIST'S REIGN FORSEEN

> **Rev.11:15-19 Says: {And the seventh angel sounded; and there arose loud voices in heaven, saying, * "The kingdom of the world has become the kingdom of our Lord, and of His Christ (Messiah) and He will reign forever and ever." * And the twenty-four elders, who sit on their thrones before God, fell on their faces and worshiped God. * "We give Thee thanks, O Lord God, the Almighty, who art and who wast, because Thou hast taken Thy power and hast begun to reign. * "And the nations were enraged, and Thy wrath came, and the time came for the dead to be judged, and the time to give their reward to Thy bond-servants the prophets and the saints (holy ones) and to those who fear Thy name, the small**

and the great, and to destroy those who destroy the earth."
* and the temple (sanctuary) of God which is in heaven
opened; and the ark of His covenant appeared in His temple,
and there were flashes of lightening and sounds of thunder
and an earthquake and a great hail storm.}

This trumpet brings to an end the first series of visions. The story of the church can only be regarded as completed when there is a final judgment upon the ages-long enemy of the gospel and the vindication of those who have been faithful through the tribulation. This passage shows a great rejoicing and worshiping in heaven. Christ, who has endured the opposition of the apostate church, finally fulfills the longing of every godly soul. He has taken His great power and started to reign. What this trumpet means the most is that the trumpet brings us just a lot closer to the end of the age. The sounding of the seventh trumpet does not refer to a momentary blast. It is rather the opposite, if is of long duration over an extended period of time. This trumpet introduces us to the pouring out of the seven bowls or wrath. This string of events brings us to the end of the world.

The bowls which are described in detail in chapter 16 begin to be fulfilled in the French Revolution at the end of the eighteenth century, but the last few await fulfillment at the coming of our Lord.

There is to be a revelation of facts associated with the temple of God. We have already shown that the reference is not the Jewish temple, which no longer exist. It is instead the spiritual temple which is the church of Jesus Christ. The thunder, the earthquakes foreshadow the commotions, revolutions, and the judgments which will take place in the fulfillment of the symbols.

"The kingdoms of this world have become the kingdoms of our Lord and of His Christ" is not a declaration that the entire earth has at this point come under forcible and conscious rule of Christ, as at the end time. But is does mean that the first great opposer is swept away, and "the kingdoms of the world" is no longer the rule and the sway belongs to Christ. Now, the kingdom was really given to Christ at His ascension. For this to happen two things had to happen. First, was the spiritual, which is the outpouring of the Holy Spirit which happened at the day of Pentecost; and the second was physical, the breaking down of the barrier of Judaism in the fall of the first great opposer. Then Christianity became a world religion.

When this happened, the kingdom of this world ended. The world Empire as well as national theocracy and its Old Testament were virtually abolished when the temple was destroyed. This marked the fact that God had setup his own kingdom, which is the fifth kingdom in Daniel's prophecy, and had begun to reign. Christianity only became a world religion, or kingdom after it became totally disassociated from Judaism in 70 A.D.

Thus, the Kingdom of God, the fifth Kingdom prophesied in Daniel becomes universal. The final dissociation of Christianity from Judaism means that it is now world wide religion. The kingdom of Christ now begins the process of encompassing and enveloping all kingdoms of the world.

This seventh trumpet brings in the final consummation of the reign of God. This is the second picture Revelation has given of the end. Here, however, there is no actual description of any judgments. The declaration of, "The kingdom of God and His Christ" seem to be the judgment here. In the song sung by the twenty four elders the Lord is simply referred to as the One who is and who was. The reason is that there is no further reason to predict his coming. The ark of his covenant seen in the heavenly temple, is mentioned here as a reminder of God's faithfulness to His covenant people who is the church.

The chapter ends with a great display of the power of God in the form of lightening, noises, thundering, an earthquake, and a great hail. This is the artillery of heaven.

APOCALYPSE
SEVEN BOWL JUDGMENTS

Time frame: The introduction of the bowl judgments in Revelation 16 tells us when they will occur. "So the first went and poured his out his bowl upon the earth, and a foul and loathsome sore came upon the men who had the mark of the beast, and those who worshiped the image." So we know from this passage when this occurs. It occurs during the last half of the tribulation period. We know because the mark of the beast, which is presented in this verse. This judgment will not be initiated until the beast assumes his place of rule over the earth. This will be at the vary mid-point of the day of the Lord. After all, this beast will rule for only forty two months of the tribulation. Therefore the time period covered by the bowl judgments consist of the entire seven year period. The trumpet judgments occur within the first half of the tribulation and the bowl judgments occur during the second half.

Historicist view has seen the final over throw of the papacy depicted in the final judgments. The language is symbolic, referring to the French Revolution and subsequent events in European history as well as some yet future which will bring down the papal power to a complete end.

Preterist position divides between those who see this as a continuation of the prophecy of the downfall of Jerusalem, and those who believe that subject was left behind in chapter 11. The latter opinion sees this section as representing God's judgment upon the Roman Empire.

Futurists find in these chapters the very end of the tribulation period, just prior to the return of Christ. Unprecedented judgments will be sent against the rebellious Satan-worshiping diehards of the Antichrist. The climax will be the final great battle of Armageddon. This will be involving millions of troops from the majority of the militarized nations of the earth. Christ will bring this war to a sudden end at His coming. **Spiritual** interpreters find a recapitulation of the trumpets series here, with an increase in intensity. These "last plagues" may be "last" in the sense of occurring at the end of time, or merely in the sense that, for certain individuals, whenever in history they occur, they are the last stroke of personal judgments from God.

> **Rev.16:1, 2 Says: {And I heard a loud voice from the temple (sanctuary), saying to the seven angels, "Go and pour out the seven bowls of the wrath of God into the earth." * And the first angel, went and poured out his bowl into the earth; and it became a loathsome and malignant sore upon the men who had the mark of the beast and who worshiped his image.}**

In view of the past this is the beginning of a series of calamities that have fallen onto the papacy and will fall again on the papacy in the course of history. God has a plan in place to overthrow the Pope. The Pope has exalted himself above God. Through out history the papacy has suffered terribly for it and God is not done yet. These are the men whom the bible refers to **"the men who had the mark of the beast, and those who worshiped his name".** This has been understood to mean "those who have sustained the secular power to which the papacy gave life and strength and from which it, in turn received the earth's fruits and protection".

The French revolution was a major player in weakening the papacy in that country. The pope at that time referred to the king of France as being one of the sons of the church. The French revolution was predicted about one hundred years previous by a Bible scholar and warned the people. But the secular powers did not listen. Then it happened. The French revolution was one of the major blows in modern history that weakened the papacy power, but it did not eradicate it entirely. France was always more significant than most other countries to sustain the papacy. The way things are in France often affected the surrounding nations, so what happened here echoed throughout Europe.

The French revolution was a foul and malignant sore. That is that the moral corruption, atheism, and the general dissolving of this society spread over those countries that supported the papacy where the beast and his image were principally worshiped.

Sore means: Causing pain or distress, severe or intense and angry. It also means an infected spot on the body. The word sore in verse 2 is associated with the plague.

The French revolution was the epidemic of atheist fanaticism. The malignant French distemper was a plague with its fanatical spirit of the new converts. This was a time when the atheist went wild. They rebelled against the papacy. The revolution was strictly aimed at the papacy. In five years two million people were slain, including 24,000 priests, and 45,000 churches were turned into stables. Then the king was beheaded. The power of the papacy was shattered in France.

The fall of Rome is also associated with this judgment. This judgment falls upon the one who carries the mark of the beast and that would be the secular government of Roman Empire, not only the government but also the loyal citizens as well. The Jews in Palestine also were apostates and carried the mark of the beast that was in allegiance with the Romans.

The new view of the apocalypse is that Jerusalem is the Egypt and Israel is the new church. This is what the Romans wanted for this area. This plague parallels that which came upon Egypt in Exodus 9:8-12. It seems mere than coincidence that this very plague was threatened against Israel when Moses was listing and counting out the judgments that he would send upon them if they proven unfaithful to His covenant. It is a fact that these sores resisted healing and can be seen in the fact that the people still were suffering from them when the fifth bowl is poured out upon them in verse 2 of Exodus 9.

The principle significance of this plague would probably be symbolic, though such literal boils and rashes almost certainly became an epidemic in the besieged city of Jerusalem where sanitation was the first luxury to be taken away. They had dead bodies piled in rotting mounds throughout the city and the streets were running with rivers of blood and sewage. It is no wonder that infections and diseases of every kind were rampant and unchecked.

These judgments follow in rapid succession. They parallel the trumpet judgments in there range of action and influence and they are more intense. The timing of these plagues would appear to be very late just before the coming of Christ.

The rashes and the malignant sores here could be the result of the tremendous pollution by radioactive fallout in the atmosphere. After the bombs were dropped in Japan during world war two, thousands of people developed hideous sores because of the radioactivity.

All internal corruption is outwardly manifested and is a sore is a vile thing to see. The sores inflicted by this plague are apparently incurable by human beings. The victims of this plague are still in torment of this plague when the fifth bowl is poured out.

In the age of many cures and medicine for everything, this plague there will be no cure. Medicine is having a hard time with some things as it is. Like Aids, for instance we see new epidemics from aids in which people cannot resist infection. Then we have super bacteria that cannot be stopped by any means. Bubonic and Ebola is rearing its ugly head. These are just the tip of the ice berg so to speak. During the tribulation there will be no cure for those who have the mark of the beast.

The trumpet judgments were just God's warnings upon the human race. The bowl judgments are God's judgments upon the human race for not heeding his warnings. Whoever refuses to be warned by the trumpets of judgments is destroyed by the bowls of wrath. For one individual a certain calamity may be a trumpet of judgment but for another it may very well be perceived as a bowl of wrath. That is the ultimate means of final destruction. "The history of the earth is the judgment of the earth". This earth is currently being putrefied.

Rev.16:3 Says: {And the second angel poured out his bowl into the sea, and it became like blood like that of a dead man; and every living thing in the sea died.}

This is the day the sea dies. Now could this mean the Mediterranean Sea or the whole world's oceans? Splitting good question. This scripture says "The Sea" There are many seas which one? This is different than ocean. Now if we look at it from the stand point that these judgments as well as all the worlds other problems are occurring in the Middle East. Then the "Sea" statement can be concentrated in this area alone. Mankind doesn't have the ability to kill everything in all of the oceans of the world, but now a smaller portion like the seas of the Middle East is a different story. This is a moot point I know. The Mediterranean Sea is right next to Israel. The United States has a fleet of ships there. There have been subtle reason why I have been hinting that these events mostly occur in the Middle East is because in the next bowl judgment, Rev.16:4 the word "they" is also the word "it". They are plural. While "it" is singular. The ancient manuscripts read "it".

In retrospect the sea would become like blood is not meant as a literal term but as imagery. This is implying that the ocean would become discolored and indicating that this was the effect of the blood that was shed in great quantities on its waters.

Since these bowls represent plagues of judgment upon the papacy the proper view point would be the complete destruction or annihilation of the naval force that contributed to sustain the papacy. France, Spain and Portugal were the only Papal nations that had a navy. The fulfillment of the prophecy is found in the series of great naval disasters that swept away the fleets of France, the most formidable naval power that had ever existed under the Papal rule.

The great naval war between France and England was in progress around the year 1793. This lasted for about 20 years with no intermission except for the short and delusive peace with Amiens in which Great Britain was strengthened by the almighty Providence that protected her to destroy everywhere the French ships, from the ships carrying commerce and the smaller colonies. This includes those of the fast and long continued allies of the French, Holland and Spain. Altogether in this naval war from the beginning in 1793 to 1815, it appears that there was destroyed between 300 to 400 frigates and an almost incalculable number of smaller ships of commerce and war. The whole history of naval warfare cannot compare to the blood shed and destruction of this war.

The term like blood does not mean blood pouring. But rather like blood. Like blood is usually meaning blood clotting. This is symbolic of putrefied by being dead already. So this is seen as symbolic. The blood of a dead man to the Jews meant to be the ultimate in un-cleanliness, so the image may simply mean that the whole nation of Judea became like the sea which is the same thing as the Gentiles Nations.

The symbolism of this passage comes from the massacres by the Romans. The Romans were notorious for slaughtering the Jews. And for such were drowning in the sea. If they lifted their heads up above the water they were either killed by darts, or caught by the vessels. If they tried to desperately escape the Roman boats they were in they attempted to swim to their enemies, the Romans either cut off their heads or their hands. They were also destroyed in other manners as well.

"Everywhere the Romans caught them until all the rest were put to flight were forced to get upon the land, while the vessels encompassed them about on the sea, but many were repulsed by getting ashore. They were killed by the darts upon the lakes and the Romans leaped out of their vessels and destroyed a great many more upon the land. One might then see the lake as bloody and full of dead men's bodies. Not one of them escaped alive. A terrible stink and a very sad sight there was the following days over that country. The shores had shipwrecks and full of dead mans bodies that are by now all swelled. They were inflamed by the sun and putrefied. They stank up the air."

The sea may also symbolize all of humanity. In view of this vision brings into focus that fact that we are living in a dead society of putrefaction. When God brings final punishment and death upon unrepentant sinners he sometimes uses the sea as an instrument. Shipwrecks, sea battles, tsunamis and other sea disasters serve as a bowl judgment. These are messengers of death upon the wicked men whose time to repent has expired while the disasters will have a different impact upon the survivors who hear of them serving as the trumpet warnings to bring them to repentance. This process has happened again and again throughout history.

This judgment may suggest the destruction of sources of physical substance which is the sea. The sea is a major source both for food and of the means of commerce.

> **Rev. 16:4-7 Says: {And the third angel poured out his bowl into the rivers and the springs of water; and they (it became) blood.* And I heard the angel of the waters saying, "Righteous art Thou, who art and who wast, O Holy One, because Thou didst judge these things; * for they poured out the blood of the saints and prophets, and Thou hast given them blood to drink. They deserve (are worthy) it." * And I heard the alter saying, "Yes, O Lord God, the Almighty, true and righteous are Thy judgments."}**

Here we have the word "They" and "it" in verse 4. Which do we look at? I like my theory better. I think all prophetic scripture is zeroing in on the only place on earth that matters in the eyes of God. The God Damn Middle East and all the God Damn shit that's destined to unfold. The ancient manuscripts are the view I favor. In retrospect we have the same view, a concentrated area only.

This judgment of the third trumpet are said to affect the rivers and the springs. In considering the third trumpet, we look for the fulfillment to be in the same region of Europe where the rivers and streams there were identified with the invasion of Attila and the Huns. So also the fulfillment of this prophecy should also be within this region of the world. The time frame of the first bowl judgments roughly coincide, all beginning with the French Revolution.

Each bowl depicts a separate aspect of the crises that came upon the Papacy at that time. France was not content to keep her revolution to her self she had to impose it upon the whole region. Beginning in 1793, France started a war with invasions against Germany, Austria, Switzerland and Northern Italy. It was the invasion of Italy that Napoleon began his career of victories from which Rome has never recovered. These wars occurred on the rivers in their respected areas. Northern Italy is abounding in rivers.

In the year 1796, Napoleon being at the age of 27 Generaled his armies across the Swiss Alps. He battled his adversaries on the rivers Po and the Rhine. It is remarkable that he won most of his battles. These regions were all Papal States and Territories.

Another part of this time period is that the Pope slaughtered many Christians in this same region. Many Christians were murdered there. The Papacy have shed the blood of the saints. The judgment upon the region is declared to be a just retribution for the shedding of their blood. It is a matter of history that in the region of the fountains of the Rhine, the Danube, and the Po rivers multitudes of saints were slaughtered at the command of the popes. These martyrs include the Lutherans, Waldenses, Vaudois, Hugoenots, and the Moravians, Hussites, and Albigens. In the times of the Papal prosecutions these valleys had been made to flow with the blood of the saints; and it seemed, at least, to be a righteous retribution that the very fountains and streams which before had been turned into blood by the slaughter of the friends of the Savior, should now be reddened with the blood of the men slain in battle.

This view of the past and in a single area is also shared again in the Middle East, this time in Israel and the Romans. This judgment is also directed against the Romans Empire and its capital city. The pollution of the water sources did occur during the siege of Jerusalem and streams of actual blood did flow through the city. This can be seen as a literal fulfillment of this vision.

Water is a symbol of life and blessing throughout the scriptures, beginning in Genesis and the Garden of Eden. In this bowl judgment the blessings of the paradise are reversed and turned into a nightmare. What was once pure and clean becomes polluted and unclean through apostasy.

The most power factor that points to this time period of 70 A.D. is the announcement in verse 6 about those upon whom calamity falls. When the third angel turns the river into blood. The angel of the waters is heard acknowledging the retributive justice of this plague. "For they have shed the blood of the saints and prophets." The killing of the prophets was the very sin of Israel and Jerusalem. There is no other nation that this crime can be alleged. This impeachment decisively fixes the allusion in this vision to the Jewish people and to that fearful period in their history when the river ran with blood.

Another symbolic approach is all the joys in life are typified by rivers and fountains of water, which are poisoned and corrupted. Even as the saints are worthy of rest and reward, so the wicked are worthy of divine chastening and judgment. The bloodletting during the Great Tribulation as saints are slaughtered by the thousands is without parallel in the history of the human race.

Judgments did fall upon the Roman Empire and judgments also fell upon the Papacy in Europe. God visits punishment in accordance with the sin committed. Once the Empires had made the blood of the saints run like water; now all the Empires can find blood to drink, and they deserve it. God's judgments are righteous. The Alter is heard speaking its agreement because it was earlier associated with the prayers of the saints for justice to be done. Part of God's answer to those cries was the sending of the trumpet judgments which were intended to warn the wicked to repent. Now in the bowls we see the final answer to those prayers, as God pours out unrelenting vengeance upon the unrepentant.

In the end time we will see the most vicious and bloody time of prosecution of believers is going to take place during this seven year tribulation period. The slaughter will be performed, not by non religious men but by religious men. These men are part of a one world religious institution.

Rev.16:8, 9 Says: {And the fourth angel poured out his bowl upon the sun; and it was given to it to scorch men with fire. * And men were scorched with fierce heat; and they blasphemed the name of God who has the power over these plagues; and they did not repent, so as to give Him glory.}

In retrospect we have Napoleon again who is the representing of the Sun Nothing escaped his heat. It is believed that the time of this vision's fulfillment overlaps the time of the second and the third bowl. This would be the years following the French Revolution, and all three focus upon some aspect of the judgment coming upon the Papal of Rome. The sun which is generally a symbol for a prominent ruler. The darkening of the sun represents either the diminishing of the power of the rulers of the papal kingdoms in general, or particularly of the power of the German emperor, who might be symbolized as the sun in the firmament of papal Christendom. Either effect can be seen to have been fulfilled in the wars of the French Revolution.

Napoleon performed the miracles of a genius. His achievements still dazzle, while they amaze the world. Within that time span of eight years he scorched every kingdom in Europe, from Naples to Berlin, and from Lisbon to Moscow. Ancient kingdoms withered before the intense blazing heat of his power. He was like the sun, there was nothing hid from his great heat. Then back to Jerusalem. There is no record of the sun's heat literally increasing to a dangerous and scorching degree at any time associated with the fall of Jerusalem of Rome. If the sun is taken as a symbol of mightily political power or a religious leader. This passage could refer to the oppression and tyranny exercised by the leader of the zealot sects that terrorized (scorched) the people inside the besieged city of Jerusalem. That is if this is the geographical and chronological setting of these judgments. But also on the other hand this could refer to Rome. If the judgment of the fall of Rome is in view, then the image may represent the tyranny of the Roman leaders or the ruthlessness of the Gothic's and Vandal kings that attacked Rome and brought about her down fall. God, in fact, threatened that the breaking of the covenant by Israel would bring upon them God's judgment in this very form: The Lord will strike you down with scorching heat. Deut. 28:22.

Then again we can take this literally. The sun is an extreme source of heat and light. This can be for man's comfort but instead this will become to man's dread and the means of his bitter suffering. If this is the case then we have to have a natural cause. One view is that of a nuclear exchange. This would be God's judgment over ruling the process of nature.

Also every now and then there are great flares of nuclear out burst outward from the sun. These flares interact with the earth's magnetic field and causes disruption in radio communication. A solar flare of intense magnitude would create immense heat upon the earth. Since we have a depletion of the O zones protective layer that is now taking place in the earth's upper atmosphere, this heat may be accompanied by an increase in ultraviolet radiation from the sun which would produce severe sunburns. A full nuclear exchange would radically alter the atmosphere. It would upset the balance of things.

How do you think things would be after a nuclear war? One of the things that would take place as a result of this nuclear exchange would be the burning up of the nitrogen in the upper atmosphere. The nitrogen would be converted to oxides of nitrogen which would then combine with and then destroy what is left of the upper earth's stratosphere. Damage to this layer can have catastrophic consequences for the earth's inhabitants. All life on earth would die. This is a brutal judgment and men still will not repent.

Rev. 16:10, 11 Says: {And the fifth angel poured out his bowl upon the throne of the beast; and his kingdom became darkened; and they gnawed their tongues because of pain, * and they blasphemed the God of heaven because of their pains and their sores; and they did not repent of their deeds.}

In retrospect we have Rome coming upon the radar again. The throne of the beast is in reference to Rome. The darkness that fills the kingdom of the beast is confusion, disorder and distress. Darkness is often the emblem of calamity.

The commander in chief of the French received his orders to storm Rome. In 1797 he received directory to advance rapidly into ecclesiastical states. The population who was in a state of unrest demanded the over throw of the papal authority. They invited the French troops to help out. The French, upon entering Rome, went about pillaging the city. The French troops ransacked the churches, the convents and the palaces of the cardinals and the nobility was laid waste. The spoiling of Rome by the French exceeded that carried out by the Vandals and the Goths. The Pope was robbed of all defenses. In 1798 he was driven out by the mobs and was ordered to dispossess himself of all his power. He refused, so he was then forcibly removed. He was dragged from the Alter, they ransacked and plundered his repositories they even took his ring from his God damn hand.

Everything in the Vatican was taken and hauled off. She was stripped naked to its walls. The territorial possessions of the church and the monasteries were confiscated and declared national property. All of the clergy were in fetters. Throughout Europe from 1798 to 1866, the authority of the papal system progressively got worse. The Pope had to flee Rome again. In the year 1848, the Pope was actually driven out of Rome who had been restored. However in 1870, the Italian troops conquered Rome and incorporated it into the kingdom of Italy.

So the fifth bowl which is about to be poured out on the seat of the beast, or the dominions which more immediately belong to, and depend on, the Roman see this judgment that probably began about 1794 and expired at about 1848 A.D. The Pope received his title in 606 A.D. and reigned till 1794 A.D. This destruction time did not destroy the papacy but it did weaken it. However, this judgment did not discourage the power of the Roman Church from perpetuating her blasphemes.

The darkness that came over the Roman Empire is the same darkness that plummeted Jerusalem in the year of 69A.D. The darkness that comes over the kingdom of Rome, which is the kingdom of the beast is a familiar symbol in the prophetic scriptures representing political turmoil and the over throw of rulers. In this time period this is what was happening in Rome. There was political turmoil. Provincial governors were stirring up disasters. Rome began to crumble from the inside.

While the first four bowls affected the forces of nature, the fifth bowl affects the political power of the beast. Judicial blindness smites this kingdom with madness and defiant rule. The throne and his kingdom are deluged with God's wrath. All becomes darkness. The boast had been "who is like unto the beast"? "Who is able to make war with him"? Well this is God's answer. Only God alone will make war with this monster. This darkness that comes upon this kingdom can be taken literally. It is also believed by some prominent believers that the black out of this future ruler will be a strategic move. By bringing darkness over this area it will allow the two hundred million Oriental troops to be advanced into the combat area on their way to Armageddon. Which is the subject of the next judgment.

The mentioning of the pain and the sores is related to the ongoing effects of the first plague. This verse shows that the first three plagues are still continuing. The sores inflicted are becoming worse. This indicates that the bowls are increasing by adding to there numbers of afflictions greatly and following in order. Despite the loss of sea life and all of nature is destroyed by this time a normal person would repent long ago. But these men will be absolute bastards at this time, because they did not repent. If they were smart they would keep their mouth shut. But no they have to go one step further. They have to blaspheme God himself.

A more modern view is that John was referring to a future revived Roman Empire. This city is the Babylon of old. The beast was born in this city and the end times he will return to the city of his birth. If this is not literal then it is symbolic. Rome is said to mean the Eternal city. This passage of scripture is referring to the beast of governmental rule in this location. Wherever it is located it will be the headquarters of this monster beast. This is undoubtedly the religious center of the world that will be put under physical darkness which is indicative of spiritual darkness. God is moving some troops around.

> **Rev.16:12-16 Says: {And the sixth angel poured out his bowl upon the great river, the Euphrates; and its waters was dried up, that the way might be prepared for the kings from the east (rising of the sun). * And I saw coming out of the mouth of the dragon and out of the mouth of the beast and out of the mouth of the false prophet, three unclean spirits like frogs; * for they are spirits of demons, performing signs, which go out to the kings of the whole world (inhabited earth), to gather them together for the war of the great day of God, the Almighty. * ("Behold, I am coming like a thief. Blessed is the one who stays awake and keeps his garments, lest he walk about naked and men (they) see his shame.") * And they gathered them together to the place which in Hebrew is called Har-Magedon (Armageddon).**

Again I would like to point out that this passage of scripture is directing things to the center of the world which is Jerusalem. I think God is not necessarily concerned with the world at large as far as the end time events are concerned. God is directing our attention to the things and the player's that are most important and that is the Middle East. God's eyes and judgments are directed in this geographical location only. The judgments are a reflection of this. The above scripture indicates that the king of the East is heading toward Armageddon by the millions. The East is meaning East of Jerusalem. This is the finality of things to come. But the earth is still in its orbit.

In retrospect the three unclean frogs signifies: 1.The spirit of infidelity coming out of the mouth of the dragon. 2. The spirit of Popery proceeding out of the beast. 3. The spirit of priest-craft coming from the mouth of the false prophet. All three of these have been manifested with great intensity in France, England, and other lands, beginning about 1830 and continued till the present day. These three spirits are paganism, the papacy, and Islam. Islam is the spirit that came out of the mouth of the false prophet, which is appropriate because of the Prophet Mohammed. The battle for the great day of the Almighty is not a real battle but just a metaphor for the conflicts of spiritual in nature in the last days. It will be the decline of Heathenism, Mahometanism, and Romanism.

However a literal interpretation is in order and that a literal armed conflict will occur of international proportions. The great war of 1914-1918 was in of itself a great Armageddon. This war convulsed and disgraced humanity.

In the year of 1917 communism was established which is believed to be one of the unclean spirits that gathers itself and the nations to the place called Armageddon. The other two spirits are Judaism and Islam. These together with communism are "all hostile to Christianity and are not reconcilable; ultimately they will war with one another into oblivion. This final war of Armageddon will be the consummation of the arms age.

It is appropriate that the fall of the last world empire be described in term of the first, since, in a very real sense it is not merely the fall of Rome, but the end of a Satanic world empire, which is predicted. This all began in Babylon, which is the head of Daniels image, and it ends with the kingdom of God, God smashes the image, and breaks it in pieces. The whole damn image falls as the stone strikes it.

On the other hand some identify Babylon of revelation with Jerusalem and therefore see this bowl judgment as related to its destruction in 70 A.D. The scene of this conflict is also Armageddon and is associated with the darkest hour in the history of Israel, the fields of Meggido, the emblem of defeat and slaughter, lies in Jewish territory. The name of evil omen was meant to be the type of that final field of blood on which Israel as a nation was doomed to perish. It is a place famous for battle and slaughter. It would mean in those days what waterloo means to us. Any great disaster to a warring nation is an Armageddon. The Confederacy met its Armageddon at Gettysburg. The Germans met their Armageddon at the Marne. Its usage here would indicate a place of great slaughter. It too is meant that Rome and the kingdom world empire in the last days will meet at Armageddon and be defeated. She is destined to go down in battle and be slaughtered.

The river Euphrates will now be completely removed, so that the kings of the east can move personal into this region to invade this land. This invasion is seen to be in connection with the sixth trumpet. The nations must gather from all four corners of the earth. They are to gather in the Palestine area. The term "Kings of the sunrise" can only mean from far eastern Asiatic countries like Japan and China. Armageddon is the judgment of the wicked nations by the Christ himself. They are gathered there for Christ to descend and then slaughter the dead nations.

There will be a coalition of nations from the Eastern countries and it will probably be led by China. There way will be cleared by the drying of the Euphrates River under the cover of darkness. This is now possible by the construction of a damn built by the Russians near the headwaters of the Euphrates.

When the Turkish power is driven into Asia Minor they will finally attempt to establish themselves in the land of Palestine. When this happens, this will arouse not only the European Nations in the leagues of the ten kingdoms, but it will stir up the eastern and northern powers as well. If prophecy is correct Turkey will be backed by Russia and possibly Germany will turn from NATO in opposition to the Western Confederation. When this takes place you can bet that the whole world will be thrown into bloody conflict. This is the time that the nations will gather against Jerusalem. These battles do not necessary mean one single event.

The nations of the world will be at this time under one world ruler or government during the tribulation. Why will the armies be gathering for war during the great tribulation while the whole earth is in such chaos? The answer is that the nations will be in anticipation for the return of Christ. They know that it is at hand and will gather their armies to stop it. All the armies will be under the rule of the Anti Christ and loyal to the beast. They will gather together at Armageddon in anticipation of the Second Coming of Christ to make war with Him and His heavenly armies. This battle that is aimed at Christ seems to be indicative of the drying up the Euphrates is symbolic of the removal of the barrier which holds back the pagan horde, the kings of the east, who join forces with the kings of the whole known world to come and do battle with the Messiah.

The next interpretation is that this final war will be one of rebellion and insurrection on the part of the many nations that do not submit to the beast and rise against the antichrist. Armageddon which in Hebrew means "Mountain of Megiddo" has been taken symbolically by some to mean, "Mount of Slaughter." This place is symbolic of the final overthrow of all the forces of evil by the might of and power of God. It also refers to the mountain that overlooks the valley of Esdraelon. This is the great plain of Jezreel in the northern part of the land of Palestine. It is an ideal slaughter ground for the armies of the world. This area, though it is a large one, is not sufficient for all the armies of the world even though the valley is fourteen miles wide and twenty miles long. This scripture is indicating that this valley is the area is a central point for the military conflict that will take place. These armies will be deployed over a two hundred mile area up and down this central location. At the time of the second coming, there will be armies in Jerusalem itself. During this time there will be great and dazzling miracles performed. The unholy trinity will have at their disposal all of the technology that mankind has created. They will be directed by Satan and dry up the Euphrates River to make way for the horde of Asians that will march under the darkness along with all of the nations of the earth will be on the march as well. They will be propelled on by the lying tongue of the doctrines of the world. The antichrist will be a desperate dog at this time because he knows that Christ will put him in prison which was just emptied already. Christ will put him in solitary confinement for one thousand years. Armageddon is his last stand. It all comes down to who has the most magic in their arsenal. Satan through man and his creations or Christ and His heavenly host?

> **Rev.16:17-21 Says: {And the seventh angel poured out his bowl upon the air; and a loud voice came out of the temple (sanctuary) from the throne, saying, "It is done." *And there were flashes of lightening and sounds and peals of thunder; and there was a great earthquake, such as there had not been since man came to be upon the earth, so great an earthquake was it, and so mighty. * And the great city was split apart into three parts, and the cities of the nations, (Gentiles) fell. And Babylon the great was remembered before God, to give her the cup of the wine of His fierce wrath. * And every island fled away, and the mountains were not found. * And huge hailstones about one hundred pounds each, came down from heaven upon men; and men blasphemed God because of the plague of the hail, because its plague was extremely severe.}**

In retrospect, this bowl is poured out into the air. This signifies a convulsion, a spoiling, invalidating and the darkening of the moral and the political atmosphere of the western nations. The thundering and the lightning represent the wars and the tumultuous situation that follows. The storm of hail indicates a judgment from the north. This suggests this could be either France or Russia. These are the most northerly of the papal kingdoms. Since the storms and the tempest seems to be coming from the air this could be referring to some supernatural cause. Then it could be meant metaphorically of the curse and devastation wrought by aerial bombardment. The effects of this bowl will be to bring down all illegitimate governments.

This bowl judgment can also be seen as applying to the downfall of the Babylon. This is meaning the papal Rome. The earthquake, the disappearance of every island and the great hail all are symbolic of the awesome and fearful character of this judgment. The division of the great city into three parts is referring to the final breaking up of the papal system which has now characterized it for nearly centuries, into a new and tri-form. This three part division is meaning that when the time comes for the total destruction of the papacy, there will be a three-fold judgment. Either a three fold judgment that comes in parts or a succession of judgments as if one part were blasted at a time happens. The same holds true for the cities of the nations will come under judgment that have been under the power of the papacy.

The fulfillment of what is stated here will be found in the ultimate overthrow of the papacy. The process described in this chapter is that of successive calamities that would weaken it and prepare it for its fall. Then there will be some tremendous judgment that would completely annihilate it and all that is connected to it.

Another view is this passage that this great city which could only mean Babylon. This statement the great city is singular and not plural. This is indicative the city of the nations. This could be nothing but the great Babylon, or the fall of Rome. The fall of pagan Rome occurred in the year 476 A.D. which would be the year of this vision fulfilled.

The other option is that the great city Babylon is symbolic for Jerusalem, and the catastrophe at is described in 70 A.D. This is when the Romans destroyed the city and massacred and deported all of the inhabitants. A number of things support this claim.

First there is the earthquake. The writer of Hebrews points out that the making of the Old Covenant was accompanied by the shaking of the earth, so it also stands to reason that the breaking of the covenant would also have an earth quake. This time both heaven and earth will shake. The Old covenant vanished away when the Roman troops destroyed the temple in 70A.D. along with the city. The city was literally divided into three parts of warring factions among the entrapped Jews. This refers to the three factions, which became acute after the return of the Romans. While they were besieging the city from the outside the three leaders from the rival factions were fighting fiercely from within. If there were no internal factions then the Jews would have been able to hold off the Roman army probably indefinitely. No army can hold out forever without supplies. The fighting within led to the fall of Jerusalem. The passage of the hail weighing about one hundred pounds could be in reference to the catapults. The catapults during this time were made with ingenuity. But these extraordinary catapults belonged to the Tenth Legion. These were the same ones that threw darts and those who threw stones. They threw them more forcible and larger that the other legions. These stones were the weight of about a talent, and were carried two furlongs and farther. The Jews could visibly see these white stones coming and hit the ground before impact. So the Romans painted them black instead. This did the job better. The impact of these stones was extremely severe.

Another view as that this bowl is poured out in the air. This is Satan's sphere. His power and dominion is dealt with in wrath. While Satan was cast out of heaven he may still maintain part of the atmosphere just above the earth, therefore holding his claim as the prince of the air.

The noises and thundering and the lighting reported in various places in Revelation we have now a great earthquake. This earth quake is unparalleled in the history of the earth. One plausible earthly explanation is this is a full nuclear exchange of all the remaining destruction weapons this earth has left. Armageddon will be in full swing at this time. Every island fled away could be referring to every spiritual religious institution that man has ever built up apart from God is utterly destroyed. It is the absolute overthrow of all civilization, and the complete wreck of man's hopes to bring in livable conditions in this world apart from God and rejecting the Lord Jesus Christ will never happen again. Everything that man has ever built will be destroyed. Those who remain will still be thinking that they can beat God and still will have nothing to do with submitting to Christ. The conclusion of this series of judgments brings us to the second coming of Christ.

It is done means that the series of plagues is completed and the judgment of God upon His enemies has reached its final manifestation. Removing every island and mountain is referring to no city even the remotest island and no fortress of the antichrist empire on a single mountain height escaped the destructive final wrath. Bowl six brings wholesale destruction. Bowl seven brings total erasure.

This is the time when the foundations of the world will be shaken and the heavens thunder judgment. It will be the time when the superstructure of a sinful planet will be utterly destroyed by God's judgments. All civilization will come to a grinding halt. The hail will sweep all the remaining earthly lies. The entire empire of evil is destroyed. It all goes down in utter ruin. Rather than repent and seek God's mercy in their final hour, the remaining reprobate inhabitants of earth will blaspheme God with their dying breath. They will speak like the demons and say damned are those who are in the heavens.

APOCALYPSE
2012

What do the Mayan calendar and the apocalypse have in common? They both have world wide catastrophic events. Both are apocalyptic. The mystical view is the Revelation along with the Scriptures. The more practical view is the destruction of all things like the Mayan vibration brings with it. Is there a difference between the two? Both are a yes and a no. They are different only in vibration. This means the feel they give off. The vibration the Scriptures gives are of a different kind than that of the 2012 vibration. The 2012 scare is more real and earthy. They are both the vibrations of the earth and signal the culmination of the end of the age.

While the four horse man already rode to the destruction of mankind during the middle (Dark) ages I do believe we are in for something far different than the four horse man. Arhiman and Satan while they are separate are in unison as to the worlds end. The worlds end is mankind's goal. This is why things are the way they are today. Today's business along with the worlds governments are in league as to the world's destruction. Ahriman's domain lives upon the European continent and extends to the Middle East. His name is known among the Muslims as Allah. Allah's personality is ridged and blood thirsty. Allah's goal is to freeze the earth rigid and this causes war. The whole continent has been ravaged with war throughout history.

Society's elite has made most everybody into walking zombies and have shut down their bodies with ill health and has shut down their thinking so that the populations cannot receive messages form the divine entities through not only ill health but through chemicals that inter the body and block the neural path ways in the brain and this stops the brain from receiving and sending signals from beyond the veil that is already in place by the spiritual dark entities of this world. This in turn weighs the soul down to the earth and we become automatons that cannot think for our selves and we cannot succeed because we are toxic in body, mind and spirit. We end up fighting with one another and eventually end up in chaos. This is the goal of the elite. Our world is over sick in every way and we all live in the transmission of illusion. If you don't believe me then all you have to do is just look around your little world and you tell me what is it that you see? If you cannot see then you too are living deep into the interior of the illusion. This illusion is the veil of the world. This is caused by believing all things world. This does not make the world bad. The world is not a bad place to live but the illusion is cosmic. It is the spiritual air that we breathe.

The year 2012 is the beginning of the illusion going away. The year 2012 is the beginning of all things new. This illusion of the world is to be put aside. A new transmission is equivalent to the Scriptures. I will pour out my spirit upon all flesh in the last days. This means a new vibration will enter the atmosphere. This in turn also means that the spirit of illusion will be done away with. In other words we humans who want to know the truth about how things really are will be the first to receive these new transmissions. So if you are reading this essay then you are in desire for new transmissions upon your soul. This report is from one who has been walking in this new transmission for the last three years and no one can understand this. Therefore I have been separated to bring this report to the world. This makes this report unique in its own right and in the category prophecy. This illusion is egoic in nature and it is the DNA of the Dragon. This DNA is fighting and will continue to struggle to survive because this earth is his and the Dragon will not give it up not without a fight. So this fight is to the death. This means total annihilation of all mankind and the world as well. If the dragon cannot have it then he will not give it up without destroying it. He will not let the regular God's have it because it is not theirs. So as a planet we are destined to go down in flames, literally!

What does this have to do with the 2012 year end date? The year 2012 is the beginning of the end of the ages. It is largely symbolic at this time in the game. The end of the ages is a process just like the Second Coming of Christ is a 2000 year process. Will the world end in 2012? Of course not. But if I want to put fear into the public I would just say of course it will. All of us will die. There I said it. How does it sound? Yes! We will all die right before Christmas how fitting is that? This is illusional at the least. This is also heresy at worst.

All these things have been predicted and prophesied since the beginning of time as we know it. We have been reminded all of our born days. This has been the talk of many a revival since time memorial. It is our religion. We are constantly being reminded in Revelation which was written with a cultic mind by the way. So was the rest of the Bible. But it is all we have to go by. The destruction of the world is at the core of our beliefs. This is not just in Christianity but throughout all beliefs systems on the world including Islam. There view of things is a bit more accurate in its own way. They are expecting a messiah called the deceiver.

All things are a process and they happen in a natural format. The year 2012 is the beginning of this process. Will the world change at that time? Of course not. Again I will ask the same question. Will the world change at that time Yes! It will change. The reason is that all things are in flux and are constantly changing anyway. But the 2012 is the signal that new transmissions and this has everything to do with the planets lining up. As the planets line up this in turn changes things on this earth. So what follows in this essay is a blue print so to speak of how all things are moving and shifting to make things happen as to the end of the age. We are indeed heading for an epic show down. Armageddon will become a UFO shoot out. Things will get worse on the one hand then on the other they will get better. We as a human race will become awaken if one desires. Right now we are all illusional and zombies. The real truth is that the earth cannot really end. After all where will the earth really go? No the earths vibrations will change. This is what the trumpets are all about. They are vibrational tones. How can we have an apocalypse without world wide droughts, city destroying hurricanes, floods, and land evasion tsunamis, along with mountains bowing their tops and record breaking earthquakes? I haven't even mentions religion destroying souls, illusional politics, and body altering chemicals along with its diseases. The 2012 hot button is beyond that. We have greater cosmic problems to add to our pathetic human equation. We have real cosmic problems coming our way. This is why no one can escape. No place on earth can one really hide. Man kind's technology boost will lead the way to bring about these cosmic events. This is man kind's goal that he may become one of the gods and enter space and gain eternal immortality without the aid of Jehovah. Can this be possible? The answer is a resounding yes it can and it has been proven. But then again this may be illusional. But nevertheless this knowledge is being publicized world wide.

There are also volcanic eruptions that are caused by solar storms, and cracks forming in the earth's magnetic field, along with the threat of mass extinctions as a result of a nuclear winter. Did I mention economic Armageddon? In addition with this we can now add massive solar flares, and polar reversals. Is it any wonder all the worlds populations are in fear about the future?

Fear is said to be false evidence appearing real. This suggests that it happens when it happens and don't even worry about it until that day. This is meaning take one day at a time and be thankful for each day you get to have. So, I propose we all sit back and watch the show as the world's leaders lead this earth to its final end. They are the one's running the show because we voted them in. How dumb they are and how stupid and naive we are. Are we living in the transmission of illusion or what? Somebody tell me I am a liar. The real question is, are we helpless? The answer is a resoundingly yes! We can do nothing to stop it. Then again I will ask this question again, are we helpless? The answer is of course not. The greater question would be is it destined? The answer is a yes! So those who decide to do something about it will be good earth citizens. We have the power to delay it only. Remember truth tellers are detested. Those who see this dark storm and inject good into it will be cut down ruthlessly. So become a warrior or sit on the sidelines. Either way we are doomed. Violence and death has been decreed until the end of days the Scriptures say. All of the gods that watch earth's activities are in agreement as to one thing only and that is the culmination of the ages. We are destined to go down in flames. **The World** We have the physical world and then we have the world of thought. In this physical world we have enemies. Right now our enemy is Islam. But they are just pawns in the larger picture. The real truth is that they are not our enemies at all but are made to look like they are. They are just human beings like you and I. Color matters not neither does religion. So we have been made to look through the eyes of disease. This indicates the disease of thought. This is splitting the thought atom. After all it is by thought we bend and shape our reality to what it is today. There will be massive change in this world. The world as we know it will massively change. Armageddon is on its way as well as total human and earth annihilation not only from within but also from without.

So in short the culmination of the ages really means not the end of time but the end of time as we know it to be. Again this is not definitive enough. I personally think it is the end of ego. So now ego struggles to survive and its goal is to keep you in illusion. It desires to bring to the world trouble and more drama. This is a signal it is judgment day for the dark ego's that run our planet. They will undergo microscopic inspection. They will come out of their dark hiding place and take over and do the devils work. This will be the signal and the beginning of the cosmic imbalances. The god's will take it from there. In this world we need to not just watch the Middle East unfold but also Europe! China, an after thought. After all this is where most of the blood of the world has been spilled. Europe's soil is blood stained by histories wars. This is why America and all other world nations are not mentioned in bible prophecy. They are all irrelevant. When Europe clashes with the Middle East then the shit has hit the fan. This is your sign. The whole world is destined to die.

What we have is a phenomenon. This is based on the proposition that cataclysmic and transformative events will occur in 2012. Cataclysmic means: violent change. Transformative means: to change in structure, appearance, or character, to change (an electric current) in potential or type. This means we are due to reach the Apex of the dramatic results on December 21, 2012 of that year. Apex means: highest point. We have reached our highest point as far as the ego is concerned and its time is up. It has had its time in not only history but also in eternity. Ego has run its course. The time of illusion is over. This is the heart of the Mayan Calendar and the 2012. This is the underlying language not mentioned in any books anywhere. This knowledge has been kept hidden for thousands of years so I could boast that this is hidden knowledge. You instinctively know this to be true. So those in Europe and the Middle East I say to you from the west Vios con dios. Go with God.

December 21, 2012 marks the end of the baktun cycle of the Mesoamerican long count calendar. The long count sets its time piece to "Time Zero" at a point in the past marking the end of this previous world and the beginning of a new one. This means not only the culmination of the ages but also the return of the god's. Does this mean the return of Christ? Yes is does. But let's throw another monkey in there. It is also the time for the return of ET'S. Human beings are Gods little monkeys. ET's see humans as stupid little monkey's. So what this is saying is that we are headed for the zero point. So the 2012 hot button is not just about the end of the ages it also represents the return of the Gods, ET's and the Abyss will open up and its eternal captives set free to roam the earth. This is why the scriptures say that those in those days will seek death and will not find it and this is because death will be upon the face of the earth. We are about to do a real life movie called 2012 culmination of the ages. Stay tuned and wait, it will come to your theater right where you are at.

One view is that we have had over 5000-6000 years since Adam and Eve. We have ended what is called baktun cycles. There are thirteen in all and each one consists of 144,000 year days each. This comes to a whopping 1,872,000 days that have gone by since Adam and Eve. The end of the world is not what the Mayans had in mind. Just because their calendar ends on that date doesn't mean the world will end. It cannot end. Think about this for a moment. Where will the world go, to hell? Don't think so. The world will be right where it's always been. It will just be a bit more screwed up but still here. So what happens next is another cycle. This cycle we can call the age or Horus. This means definitely a long time. It will signal the end of this age and at the same time issue in another age. This one will bring with it savagery and cosmic intelligence at the same time.

As we ask ourselves why December 12, 2012? It is believed that the Mayans fixed their calendar to end on the winter solstice in sequence of the cosmic alignment would maximize. The Mayans did not make this calendar, but some Olmec High Priest about 236 B.C. No man monkey upon himself can see into the future 2300 to 5000 years into the future all by himself. He has to have some help from either a dark or higher force or ET'S. Can you see into the future 5000 years from now, of course not I rest my case. This is not the natural course of slave minded and diseased oriented stupid man.

With the invention of stupid nuclear smart bombs and wild and tricky technology we will see cataclysmic events as well as a spiritual revival that will be both cosmic and destructive at the same time. The end and the beginning happening simultaneously. This will be marked by significant changes physically and spiritually and mentally. I even predict even a restoration of the true balance between the divine masculine and feminine energies. We can anticipate a change in the nature of consciousness of course assisted by indigenous insights and psychedelic drugs use. This to me sounds like a license to do mushrooms and drop some acid and trip on things. By doing this only can we start to see things in their true light. The reason is simply because consciously things make no sense. The base reason for the 2012 hot button is the Mayan calendar. Time as we know it comes to an end and a major shift in human consciousness occurs for those in the earth who can receive new transmissions from the cosmos. We are entering a time for the return of the gods. This concept is biblically based in addition to the new age of reason. There is alignment and they run parallel to each other.

Let's add in another view here for great measure. Let's say that it is also believed that there will be a shift that will reveal the 4th dimension which is time and maybe the 5th dimension and that is to become one with the spiritual world. This means that we will enter a time where heaven and earth will meet together. If this is true then our egos must be removed. This is also biblically based in the apocalypse. This is what is happening heaven comes down right after hell has unleashed its demonic army force and to get things started man will kick of the game through world war. So this means that the return of the god's concept is also the culmination of the return of Christ and His heavenly host. The return of Christ and His Heavenly Army will be coming to earth in judgment. Spirit guides think we will be able to see inanimate objects and that animals will speak to people in our native tongue to prove God's dominion on this earth.

Planets Let's throw another monkey wrench in here for great measure. First we will have a geomagnetic reversal of the earth. This means that our magnets that now point north will now point south. How odd is that? The last time this happened was about 800,000 years ago. Christian believers don't even believe this ole earth is that old? I personally think that this earth is a lot older than that. It is believed with absolute certainty that this will happen in 2012. I do not believe this for one minute. Don't ask me why because I cannot tell you. The certainty crowd suggests that the earth's magnetic reversal is connected to the natural eleven-year solar cycle. But there are those that think this hogwash. There appears to be a current downtrend in magnetic field strength. The current magnetic field is still considered to be above average. When compared with the variations measures throughout history. The current magnetic field is healthy and will more than likely continue in strength with its pattern of natural fluctuations as it has over the last 5000 years. The dipolar field would continue to decrease at the current trend and would effectively be returned to zero in a few hundred years time. There is also confusion concerning polar reversal, polar shift and geomagnetic reversal. These three are not the same. A polar reversal is horror. This is when the pole shift and that the axis of rotation of the planet has not always been at there present day location and this means that the poles have been shifted. The results would be a world turned upside down. Life after a polar shift would be the end of all life on this planet. It would result in unmanageable horror. The securities that we have come to know like food, water and medicine would come to a halt. All securities would come to an immediate stop. This is the beginning of chaos. The civilizations of the world would start to vanish. It is the most horrifying nightmare you can imagine. It would be more devastating than a nuclear holocaust that has been unleashed. We cannot imagine what the mess would be like. This is truly annihilation of the whole world.

Venus is one planet that has a polar reversal and look what that has done for love. Love has been turned upside down. Love today is completely perverted. This is because Venus has been flipped upside down and has been in reverse. Venus rotates in the opposite direction from all the other planets. It was flipped upside down by some huge event, such as a planetary collision.

Again we have Uranus. This planet rotates on its side. This would explain why we have sideways people. Uranus has been knocked off its axis by some sort of impact, or maybe some gravitational effect probably caused by Jupiter and Saturn. What this is saying is that there is little evidence that a polar reversal will take place in 2012 unless Lucifer's hammer (Nibiru) gets knocked off course and out of orbit. This would be very bad indeed.

Another bad idea set forth by the 2012 proponents of planetary annihilation is the twisted alignment of the planets. This seems to be right on with the Maya calendar. I am sure this is the picture they were looking at when they made their predictions. They were sun worshipers. They noted that the sun will be in the center of the galaxy with all the planets aligning. Who can survive except the well prepared? Also when this alignment occurs then the energy that earth receives from the center of the Milky Way will be disrupted on December 12, 2012. This planetary alignment disruption has been predicted from 1990 all the way to 2020. This is a time period indeed. This makes more sense than a simple date. There is no instability to the inner earth's core at this time. The Mayans were Sun worshipers and they knew that the Sun travels in an orbit through the galaxy just as the planets of the solar system travel in an orbit around the sun. Yet at the same time they also believed that the earth was flat. Go figure. They did not get their knowledge by themselves. They had dark forces at their aid. Perhaps their maker E.A and Company were camping out with them. How can an ancient people with no aid of technology know the deep things of astrology? I cannot personally give them credit to anything. The credit goes only to the ones who have this ability. Like I said before mankind is a diseased slave that does not know shit by them selves. You have to have supernatural powers at your aid to know that the earth is round and that it has axis.

Next we have the nay Sayers and they say that the planets will not be anywhere close to this kind of alignment at this time. The chances of this kind of bad alignment can happen only once in eighty six billion, trillion years. So what are the odds? The odds are that an exact planetary alignment will never occur throughout the entire history of the solar system. So what do we have here are opinions that have no bases in reality. These are what we can call heresies. We have truth and lies. We also have those who are not well informed. I too consider myself not well informed. I know that I don't know. When we have disagreement then we have discord. Who can you really listen to? I say listen to everyone and then listen to know one and just observe reality. Reality always wins.

Then we have Planet X. Planet X is the big question. What is Planet X? Planet X is also known as Lucifer's Hammer. It is considered a rogue planet. Actually it isn't even a planet. It is a huge rock about the size of earth and that is predicted to go astray at any time. The Mayans knew about this rock because their creator E.A. @ company told them about it. They also believed that this rock will doom the earth in 2012. This is why they ended their calendar at December 12th, 2012. This rogue rocks name is Nibiru. NASA has been tracking this rock for at least forty years. Because they also believe that this thing is rogue they keep quite about it. The proponents of the 2012 events believe as true that Planet X will pass by the earth in 2012. When it passes by it will create whether storms out of balance with nature. This will cause severe whether patterns. Then there is the belief that planet X will collide with the earth knocking earth off its axis. The Mayans of course are not the only ones who knew about this rogue planet. The Sumerians also knew about it. Now who do you think told them? E.A @ company told them. E.A. seems to be the creator of all the earths colored race that is not Jew. This knowledge about this Planet X was recorded on the Sumerian tablets that identified that the planet Nibiru orbits the Sun every 3600 years. This info is used by writers and psychics to scare the pants off of everyone and its working.

In the year of 1983 the Washington Post ran an article about this rogue planet and this is why we know for certain that this knowledge was available since that time. So mysterious is this planet that astronomers can't tell if it's a rock or a planet, a giant comet, or a protostar that never got hot enough to become a star. A distant galaxy so young that is still in the process of forming its first stars, or a galaxy so shrouded in dust that none of the light cast by its stars ever gets through. The news paper at this time did not indicate that the mystery mass would collide with our planet. Let alone the projected date of 2012. If it does then it would produce cataclysmic events so terrible that we dare not even think about it. We now latch onto this story and we add fear in the mix now we have a world phenomenon. Remember the gods are in control. Nothing happens in this world unless the gods say so. The end of the world is a controlled con that is destined to become real one way or another. We can predict our future with accuracy by creating our future actively. All action is wrought by thought. Let's all add more bricks to this fear. I am all for chaos. What can you do about it? Nothing, except to find yourself a perfect beach life somewhere and enjoy each and every moment of your lives creating great eternal memories.

Now that we have a small blue print or snapshot of this hot button 2012 question, we can also go to the scriptures for other info and help us get a larger picture of things. The reason is because there is complete void of scientific evidence for the theory that December 12, 2012 will end the world as we know it. Although there are pretty good arguments on both ends of the spectrum they are all valid to a certain point and we will only know for sure by waiting to see what takes place and we get what we get. The reality will unfold when it's supposed to.

This does not mean that things will occur on this date. God has answered for us this equation in His word. In fact He provided us with the Book of Revelation along with the rest of the Bible and its containing prophecies. This includes the seven year period of the tribulation than will not be far different than the one predicted here. Prophecy does not spell out exactly what will occur but only that it will happen and that it will be the culmination of the ages.

Let's examine this for a moment. What do you think God has in mind for a world wide catastrophic calamity? Let's just say a little bit of everything for starters. The 2012 blueprint is a snapshot of God's judgment upon this ole bad earth and all of the inhabitants. Man kind along with the blessings of the fallen gods will go on a world wide campaign to rid the world of the mystical mind set. This is automatic world war and will cause massive chaos alone. This is the criminal mind set that is our excuse for our failure. The mystical mind set is the ego all in a nut shell. So therefore we have to say all this is about the God damn ego. What this is saying is that this God Damn ego will die and the earth is destined to go down with it. The ego will not go out without a fight to the death. The ego you remember is the Dragons Nuclei Atom that is super glued to the human soul. This is his claim upon all humanity. The regular God's have given it time in eternity. The DNA's time is about up so it goes stir crazy. This is the reason for the antichrist. He is the king of ego and E.A's personal agent he is here to save all egos from God's wrath by going to war with them. God will use these events for the end time fulfillment of prophecy. He will use natural things along with the natural process of things to pull it off. The scriptures are in alignment with this theory. A violent end is decreed and war by mankind until the end of time.

God has shown us what will come upon the world 2000 years ago. Also remember the Second Coming of Christ is in the now. We are living in the Second Coming of Christ. The second coming is not a one time event it is a process. All of the heavens are going to be disrupted to stop this actual coming because this earths dark creators time is about up. But heaven is up against the death dragon. E.A is not called the death dragon for nothing. Churches have been preaching the second coming for 2000 years now. The culmination of the ages is the 2012 hot button. Things are building up on a world wide scale. All of the world's armies are not yet ready but they are still perfecting their technology. This is their time. Their time for developing will be up soon and mankind will kick off the game and this will be your sign. Even though it will all come too soon it will be in God's good timeframe. So the world will not end at this date but things will happen that is for sure.

God's Revelation of this future era is a compelling and stunning account. Read the rest of the Apocalypse for the whole story. This near future period will bring such a change to the earth that at its beginning the world as we know it will end. Tell me, how did you like Katrina? Well! There you have it. We are already in the apocalypse. From this point it is just a matter of intensity. We are already experiencing the apocalypse in slow motion. Kind of like a divorce. A process of a divorce starts well in advance before the actual divorce. The division of souls happens when there is a split in the thinking process. Once that split happens then the unhappiness occurs. When the unhappiness occurs then the parting of ways will eventually happen it is just a matter of time. So the spirit of divorce is the power that works behinds the scenes and is ever present in the marriage. But its time comes when its time comes. So the apocalypse is ever present and the forces are ever getting larger under the surface. We all feel it. It will come when the powers that be determine it will come. Again nothing happens on this earth unless it's predestined. The culmination of the ages is the agreement of compromise of the gods. The culmination of the ages is destined to become the eternal God Damn Rock the Earth and

Heaven's hell unleashed show down that eternity will never forget and hell will respond.

Mankind has large ambition. Mankind must fulfill his destiny and become one of the god's. It is man's supreme ambition. All things must die in the process except this time it is not just about world war 3. If world war 3 happens and that is all we have then we can consider our selves lucky. In the mean time find your appreciation for the little things and live a great life while you have the ability as God has granted you life. The god's can be considered ET's. Harmony and convergence will not happen upon this earth until the consumption of the era is complete.

Planet X (Nibiru) is considered the twelfth planet. Nibiru is on an elliptical (oval) orbit, which enters the solar system every 3600 years and it is believed that it is populated by the Annunaki, who are the Biblical Sons of God dejected from heaven. The Annunaki means those from the heavens came. In the book of Enoch they are referred to as the watchers. It is believed by some that the watchers and Planet X were responsible for the disasters in Exodus, as it shunted dangerously close to earth and mars. This is what triggered the eruption at Thera. Again around the year 700 B.C a large passing body probably interfered with the planet Jupiter and this cause the ejecting of Venus. The next return of Nibiru is due between 2012 and 2036. During this time between now and then it will become more visible to earth and will appear as a new star. Nibiru is also recognized in old Babylon myths.

RELIGION

Rapture and 2012 There are those who get on the internet and yell all sorts of stupid things like the Second Coming of Christ in 2012. This of course is so not going to happen. There are other things that must take place first like me seeing my children grow up. Then there is the trivial things like the nations are not technologically ready for war. They say the day of the Lord will arrive. Well they forgot about the antichrist. The day of the antichrist will happen first. So the day of the Lord will be the same day as the antichrist. If this is true then this suggests that the regular God has sent the antichrist to punish this world and make war and desolation. This then is the will of God that this takes place. This of course is the one world governmental body. So in essence the day of the Lord is the day of the antichrist. This also could mean that this is the day of ET's return. I am sure these people are wearing hoods and calling them selves the group of Natas Reficul. They will also be calling for a one world order. In the last days of this world I think I will do the same. I might be on the internet wearing a black hood saying things like ET's are coming, the ET's are coming.

When it comes to religion we have all sorts of views that can be taxing and out of them all comes uncertainty. Groups like the post, and the pre millennialism, the millennialism, then we have the post tribulation crowd and then we also have the pre tribulation crowd. I can just about guarantee they are looking at prophecy through the lens of chaos and uncertainty. The reason is pretty simple. I certainly believe that the Bible is written in code and this is something we can all agree on. But to go deeper I believe that the Bible is written with an occultist mind. So to understand it we too have to have an occultist mind set to decode. Otherwise we cannot see deeper to its inner meaning. In the Christian Community I am all alone in this view. Therefore I do not fit their mold. Due to this fact this is now my unique position. I personally embraced all other beliefs systems to add to my internal knowledge bank and this has broadened my perspective and enhanced my deeper psychic. My astral vision has sky rocketed far past the moon and the stars as a result of the action.

Let's see if we can find any reason why concepts such as the rapture, The Second Coming of Christ and Judgment day are being connected with 2012. These various approaches mentioned above can be summarized by saying, that there are biblical reasons for expecting the seven year tribulation (times of distress) and that either before or after or halfway through this period the Rapture will take place. This is when millions upon millions (chosen ones will be taken up into the clouds en-route to the heavenly places to spend eternity. Judgment day will then ensue forward now that the hostages are snagged from the devil's snare. This will occur before the tribulation and then the next one will happen after the tribulation. Then we have those who think that the Rapture will not take place until one thousand years after the return of Christ.

Fundamentalist preachers state that the Second Coming will happen between 2001 to 2012. Well this has not taken place as of yet. Good luck in predicting the next one. What we do have is the Gospels of Matthew, Mark, Luke and John. Then we have the prophet Daniel. This is considered Judaism beliefs.

Gospels Most people assume that the end time prophecy starts and ends with the book of Revelation. This is the last book in the Bible and is still to this day not an open book that is easily decoded. But the thinkers are getting a bit smarter. When they figure out the occultist equation then they will get it into higher gear and maybe figure it out with accuracy. The book of Revelation is not the only book with prophecy encoded about the apocalypse.

Matthew chapters 24 and chapter 25 describes a mini apocalypse. Matthew we have the **Signs of Christ's Return.** Then we have the **Perilous Times**, Then there is The **Glorious Return,** The **Parable of the Fig Tree,** Then we have **Be Ready for His Coming.** In chapter 25 we have The **Parable of the Ten Virgins, Parable of ten Talents.** Then we have **The Judgment of the Nations.**

Next on the list is **Luke 21:24 Which says: {and they will fall by the edge of the sword, and will be led captive into all nations; and Jerusalem will be trampled underfoot by the Gentiles until the times of the Gentiles be fulfilled.}**

This prophecy was fulfilled in 68-70 A.D. This is the time when the Romans destroyed their temple. The Jews had to wait another 1900 hundred years to be able to regain Jerusalem. This was accomplished in the 1967 six day war. At which point 'the times of the Gentiles' which means non Jewish people were fulfilled. This version in Luke 21:24 goes onto describe the physical, religious and moral signs that would take place between the first sign, or the pre-sign, in 1967 and Jesus' return. Most educated believers think that these signs have now been fulfilled. I agree.

Next we have in **Luke 21:29-33 Which Says: {And He told them a parable: "Behold the fig tree and all the trees; as soon as they put forth leaves, you see it and know for yourselves that summer is near. * "even so you, when you see these things happening, recognize (know) that the kingdom of God is near.* "Truly I say to you, this generation shall not pass away until all things take place. * Heaven and earth will pass away, but My words will not pass away.}**

The Biblical generation is said to be three score and ten years this comes to 70 years. So from 1947 or 1948 we add 70 years to this and we come up with the year 2016. Let me be stupid here and say that the world will end in 2016. There you have my stupid and dumb prediction. I hope it will not come to pass though. My kids are not old enough yet. I want grand kids you know. The nation of Israel was reestablished in the year of our Lord 1948. Prophecy fulfilled. Now to add another twist to this equation we have the abomination of desolation which actually happened when the Jewish home land was reestablished. From the Islamic stand point the Jews are the abomination of desolation. This is why they are called Little Satan. The United States is the Big Satan and the land of Babylon. But another view is that the abomination of desolation was to be set up on the temple Mount on December 12, 2012 then 1335 days later would bring us to the date of August 2016. This would be considered seven weeks of years from the 1967 year. Now we have another Date for Judgment. This is only one prediction from using the wisdom of man. Pretty good isn't it?

Ezekiel The book of Ezekiel contains a precession code. Precession meaning: slow circling of the rotation axis of a spinning body. This has been interpreted to signify that this precession code ends around the year 2144 A.D. This is the time when the spring equinox rotates into Aquarius. From the years 1945 to 2012 figures hard in this time period. This is supposed to be the time when gog was destroyed but we know this has not happened. But they did take a licking in Afghanistan. Gog is mentioned in Revelation as well as Ezekiel 38, 39. Gog and the destruction of gog covers two chapters. This indicates that the years 2000 to 2012 is the extinction of humanity. So these predictions were inaccurate once again. Between these two periods the black horse of death out of Revelation was supposed to happen but I didn't notice it did you. So now the prediction again that the pale horse will ride the earth between 2013 to 2016. These are bad predictions at best. These are worldly predictions by those who are very educated and smart. In truth they were done by monkey's.

The Mayas and the Jewish Torah agree on one matter and that is that creation happened over a 6000 year stretch. Not the seven days like Genesis states. This makes Genesis inaccurate. This Bible's verbology sets the stage for what is in the pages to follow, more inaccuracy. The Jewish interpretation is better and makes more sense. Christian dogma dictates that the world was created in six days and rested on the seventh. This is symbolically true. So the Bible speaks symbolically. Symbolically means: something that represents or suggests another thing. But the Torah also states that a macro cosmic creation event extending through history. These two beliefs align. The Torah also teaches that there were 7000 years of time during the creation process. This is the 6000 years followed by the 1000 years Messianic Kingdom.

In **Psalms it Says:{For a thousand years in Thy sight Are like yesterday when it passes by, Or as a watch in the night.}** The Jewish calendar starts with the birth of Adam. Adam was born in 4004 B.C. 6000 years later we would arrive in 1997. The Jews also believe that the Rosh Hashanah between the years 1999, and 2012 is the 6000 years of years completed since creation. This is the 6000 years of man. After this 2012 date the Jews believe that this signifies a new millennium. What this means for the modern world is that we are on borrowed time. The seven years of Adam and Eve creation and their eating the delusional fruit from the tree of stupidity has to be pre-figured in there as well. Either way we are in deep dodo. So if we back up seven years this brings us to 2005 to 2007 A.D. either way we look at these figures the 2012 seems to pop on the radar screen. The Jewish also believe that Rosh Hashanah is related to heavens gate opening and we will enter by rapture and then along with that they also believe that heavens gate will close on September 26, 2012 and celebrate this event by a festival called the Yom Kipper. Yom Kipper is also related with the return of the Messiah. **Daniel** In the book of Daniel he makes a comment that "seventy weeks of years." This represents 490 years of time. This is encoded symbolism. Seventy times seven equals 490 days.

> **Daniel 8:13-14 Says:{Then I heard a holy one speaking, and another holy one said to that particular one who was speaking, "How long will the vision about the regular sacrifice apply, while the transgression, causes horror, so as to allow both the holy place and the host be trampled?" * And he said to me, "For 2,300 evenings and mornings; then the holy place will be properly restored."}**

The Greek invaded Israel around the year 333 B.C. Alexander the Great captured the city of Jerusalem in 332 B.C. It is from these dates that we add 2,300 days of years rule and we come up with 1967. Give or take a couple of years. Since these calculations fails to account the missing zero point between the B.C and the A.D dates. There is however a direct connection to the words of Jesus when Daniel overheard a holy one of an ET asks how long the sanctuary would be "trampled underfoot."

> **Daniel 12:11-13 Says: {"And from the time that the regular sacrifice is abolished, and the abomination of desolation is set up, there will be 1,290 days. * "How blessed is he who keeps waiting and attains to the 1,335 days. * But as for you, go your way to the end; (end of the age) then you will enter rest and rise again for you allotted portion at the end of the age." (days)}**

The last three verses of this chapter it indicates the 1,290 and the 1,335 days of years. There is 45 years difference. Perhaps there will be buffer of activity when it happens between these two dates. But then again 45 years after the 1967 reestablished date brings us to 2012. There it is again this 2012 date. It is beginning to pop up on the radar screen.

Around the year 597-602 B.C. Jerusalem fell to Nebuchadnezzar. This is about the time the burnt offering was done away with. So 1,290 years later the Dome of the Rock was built on the Temple Mount on or near 691A.D. This would be considered the "Abomination of Desolation" scripturally speaking. This is the abomination as far as the Jews were concerned. So this means that the abomination of desolation was set up and the burnt offering was done away with at this time. Now remember the Muslim god is not Jehovah. If they had the same God then there would be total harmony, but we know this is not the case. The god Allah is Ahriman who is the god of the Muslims. Ahriman's personality is hard and rigid and he rules by the sword (force). This is his personality trait. This is why that he is considered an abomination from desolation and will cause desolation. So we now have two interpretations of what the abomination of desolation is. The Dome of the Dock is an abomination to the Jews and the Jews are the abominations to the Muslims. So in essence they both are abominations. This is the definition of hate. This goes back to the twin brothers born of Isaac the son of Jacob who was the son of Abraham. To add another insult to this mix is that there is rumored that there was a previous mosque on the site of the Dome of the Rock. This had a suggested construction date of 667 A.D. So now 1,290 years later would bring us to the 1967 date where prophecy was fulfilled. Then we add another 45 years to the 2012 date.

Revelation The nations have trampled upon Israel and its beloved God city Jerusalem. The nations will trample and have trampled over this city for over 4000 years. There must be a great reason why this is so. The scriptures only give hints here and there and they are all in symbolic code and are not definitive enough. Trample means: Thresh, to walk or step on so as to bruise or crush. The 1,290 figure appears in Daniel twice and it appears in revelation once in the form of 42 months. 42 times 39 comes to 1,290. This is also known as time, times and two times and a half. This is based on the 360 days a year. 93x360 and then add 180 comes to 1,290 years.

The other view is that the 1,260 year is tied to the feast of trumpets which is the Rosh Hashanah of the Jewish year of 2005. This starts at sundown on October 3. It is supposed to occur on the day of Tishri in the

Hebrew calendar. On this date there occurred an annular solar eclipse. This also means that there was an interval of exactly 2,550 days before the Yom Kipper in 2012. The Yom Kipper is known as the great Trumpet, and this occurs in September 26, 2012. So now we add 1,260 to 1,290 and come up with the figure 2,550. This is negative A.D. 79. This is about the time Jerusalem was trampled or threshed. But also on the other hand if we come from the September 26, 2005 stand point and add 2,550 days we would come to august 28, 2012. This is manufacturing evidence, is it not? This is called manipulation. I like it let's do some more.

What this is saying in Jewish terms is that the 2005 date is the date the sign of the heavens occurred as outlined in Revelations.

> **Revelation 12:1,2 Which Says: {And a great sign appeared in heaven: a woman clothed with the sun, and the moon under her feet, and on her head a crown of twelve stars; * and she was with child; and she cried out, being in labor and in pain to give birth.}**

The cosmic interpretation or the astrological interpretation would be as follows: The Moon would be at the feet of Virgo. This is one of the twelve constellations, with the Sun at her shoulders and Jupiter and Mercury in her belly. It is expected a red comet to pass by at this time. If so, then this would be your sign and in concert with the Red Dragon that is talked about in Revelation. This is the start of the seven year tribulation period. If this is the case then the end of the tribulation would end on October 2012. After that we would go to the start of the next millennium and this would be the end of the current age and the new age of Horus. After this we look forward to the alignment of Venus with the star of Regulus, which is at the foot of Leo. This will correspond to several Bible passages. So again we have scripture speaking in symbolic terms only that are not easily decoded.

> **Revelation 2:10 Says: {Do not fear what you are about to suffer. Behold, the Devil is about to cast some of you in prison, that you may be tested, and you will have tribulation ten days. Be faithful until death, and I will give you the crown of life.}**

This scripture is definitely indicating calling this a test with the reward of the crown of life upon passing this death test. So here we are encouraged to be happy little lambs and be willing to be slaughtered.

No where in Revelation is seven years mentioned. This "seven years" is an assumption based in Daniel 9:24-27. If the day equals a year rule then this would be ten years tribulation. This is pointing the way for the coming of the Messiah.

In the year of 2005, is the year of the arrival of the Electrical Magnetic Pulse (EMP). Seven years later we again come to the 2012 date. Can we conclude this as manufactured evidence of is this conjuring and looking for things that coincide here? I personally think all of the above. If it happens on October 3, 2012 then this would coincide with the feast of the tabernacles in the Jewish calendar. This is also known as the Sukkot. This is the celebration of the end of the harvest. But on October 4, 2005 there were no red comets. But we did have a Kashmir earthquake that killed about 80,000 people. We also had 1,260 people killed by a massive hurricane that hit Mexico of that year.

Islam and 2012 From the Islamic point of view the United States is the new Babylon. This makes Israel and the gaining of Jerusalem the Abomination of Desolation which includes the United States. All three of these religions are destined to clash. Islam who's god is Ahriman, Judaism, who's God is "I am" and Christianity who's God is Christ. These are three distinct personalities. This is holy war. This is what Armageddon is all about. But not what sparks the world war. That is a whole other subject. The earth will be embroiled in war only as a preparation for the Second Coming of Christ because of the Second Coming of Christ. Man kind will go through testing to see if he can take on the heavenly host of Christ's army. So at Armageddon the best of the world's best will be there, winner take all. Today each one of these powers has a holy war attitude already. This is all under the veil of illusion and delusion. Through heresies will this be accomplished. This indicates deception at a diabolical level.

Armageddon is a set up for mankind's army of opposition to be slaughtered. But this is the battle for earth and the powers over it. So all this is saying is that all events that we are trying to calculate are the side roads to Armageddon. But all these stupid events must happen to get there nonetheless. But the powers that be don't look at it that way. They look at this like this is something that has got to be done. It is their destiny, and they are driven to this end. They are being used willingly. They are also predestined to perish.

The times of distress and the times of blessings is another view here. The times of blessings was started in 1967 with the reestablishment of Israel Then add 45 years and the date is 2012. This is the signal for the times of distress. Now remember this is the world's wisdom which is folly to God.

The Islamic end day is called the year of the Haj. The year for this end date is 2076. This does mean the end day. The reason is that this aligns with the 1500 year Islamic calendar. The greatest Islamic minds also agree that the end date is 2076. This is there mind set and there is no adding or subtracting from this. No one knows the day except Allah. (Ahriman) Like Judaism and Christianity, Islam also expects a last day that is considered a judgment day. This is known among Muslims as mala" ika which is angels. They have names like Mikail which is Michael and they also have a Jibril which means Gabriel. There is also an evil Jinne that we call genie. This genie is an earth spirit and his name is Shayton.

At the death of a Muslim, the ruh (spirit) goes to purgatory after it leaves the body. The spirit enters into Barzakh (purgatory). After that it returns to the body on Yawn nas-Ba'th. This means the return from the grave.

This corresponds smartly with Revelations, the anti-christ will rise from the grave imitating the three day in hell that Christ went through. This is why we will think he is god. But this rise from the grave will probably be the long lost Caesar.

Barzakh is for Muslims only. Therefore from the Christian stand point this is not heavenly. This must be the town and street location in another place other than heaven as we know it. We can also conclude along these lines that this must be somewhere located in hell. But to soften this stance a little bit let's just say it is probably somewhere in the underworld. We can also conclude at this time that is the Catholic Religion identifies themselves with purgatory then they also are spiritually connected with this underworld called Barzakh. This connects them with the Muslim death location. So the Anti Christ comes from or stems from the Babylon religions which are heavily connected with the Muslim faith under the surface of it all. But on the surface they are neither connected but appear opposites. Yet they are destined to clash. This is the world's clash of the Titans. Now get this they are also expecting an anti Christ with open arms. His name is Dajjal. His name means deceiver. He will come and try to kill the returning prophet Jesus as he returns. But this Jesus will kill Dajjal. But this Jesus is nothing more than a great prophet. Allah Bless them for that. Allah is good. All Muslim thinkers regard prophecy and predictions as a really bad idea. So Dajjal is the anti-christ himself. He is said to be already alive and waiting to make an appearance.

Bible code The Bible code is the new computer generated mystical way of seeing into the future as well as the past. It alone is a phenomenon. This discovery was impossible before the computer age. This takes special software that decodes the Bible by applying a skip method to the whole text. This is done by skipping a certain number of letters, then extracting a letter then repeat the process over and over again until you get a message. They do this in the old Hebrew Old Testament. This helps predicts all major news items, from the holocaust to Hiroshima. This new technology is now predicting the asteroid that wiped out the dinosaurs sixty five million years ago. It has not mentioned any more asteroids. Now they are saying that the Jewish calendar year 5766 which is the year of 2005 to 2006 has been found to encode the word comet, it struck their dwelling. Another prediction was in the Jewish year of 5770 which is our 2009 it says comet with the words horror, along with darkness and gloom. And to make matters worse the Jewish year 5772 which is our year of 2012 it reads. Earth annihilated. But none of this has happened. Now that last thing that was predicted is in the Jewish year of 5774 or 2014 predicts great terror and an asteroid. The year 5873 or 2113 reads great terror, fire, earthquake, empty, depopulated. Then the year 5886 or 2026 which is its last date it reads it all happened in the seventh month. This coincides with what the astronomers have predicted about the comet swift-Tuttle. It is due to arrive in the year 2026.

This really is all too much to take for us humans. But Revelations does in fact prophecy the end of days and all the major world religions agree. Now science is verifying in it in their own monkey way. The bible code did also predict the 9/11 tragedy which was encoded in the book of Exodus along with the name Bin Laden. So far the Bible Code goes up to 2010 and this was the predicted date of World War three. Now we know that this has not taken place either. So what are we to conclude about all of this worldly wisdom? Not much actually, all predictions were made by man monkeys. What the powers that be want is a lot of hype so that we are all running around scared and its does in fact work. I too am largely scared. I will find my self a cave and hide and stock up on supplies for a long time and do not ever want to see civilization again. Then that is not a great idea because then the mountains will fall on me. I think there is no place better to survive than next to the mall where there are a lot of supplies in case things go bad. Live in the heart of the big city, where there are grocery stores, clothe stores and car lots. Big box stores are nothing more than supply houses just waiting and are ripe for raiding.

All of these predictions and prophecies have one common thread and that is the year of 2012. Oh! There is more but don't you just love a great story?